Into Glorious Light

A Memoir

by Paul Keough, PhD, MBA

Into Glorious Light: My Memoir of Converting from Exhausted Atheist to Joyful Christian

ISBN: 9781796297317

Photo of the Shakespeare Garden courtesy Mary Ann Grumman

Table of Contents

Dedication

My memoir is dedicated to the hope that atheists, agnostics, those struggling with faith, and those who do not yet know God may also gleam some seed of truth from this book on their path into glorious light.

Foreword

Larry is one of my former students who now excels his teacher. Larry has edited parts of the text with poignant brilliance to the point that I thought that he would be a good person to introduce this memoir. As the author of the book, I do not think I should comment on a foreword at the risk of damaging the free expression of the editorial itself. The journalist must be free to express what he saw himself in the book - for that is the most important thing. I hope that somehow this book will end up in the hands of atheists, and of those atheists, that earnest consideration enters their minds and hearts to consider the truth of the Christian, living God.

Paul Keough, author

In this foreword, I try to speak to both atheists and Catholics. People do a lot of writing and talking about themselves: the blog of a college friend, a politician's memoirs before they run for president and parents' stories of 'back in the day'. If the person interests you, you listen. If they went through similar things to you, then there is possibly an alchemical, transformative moment of catharsis, or, at least, the uplifting comfort of not being alone and knowing a bit more about how to navigate the world and survive. But it's not easy to tell people about one's real, humbling life.

Paul Keough writes his life's story well. He writes of the vast distances his soul has passed over. Throughout his telling, Paul shares his thoughts and feelings at different stages of his life, and the style formed by this extreme introspection is like role-playing past versions of himself that still live inside him in the present time. This is not an easy process. We can see that Paul is a bit of an ascetic—someone who practices severe self-discipline. Running the gauntlet of painful memories, he treats himself poetically, juxtaposing different memories and stories. These are not so much knit together by abstract reflections on motivations and desires, so much as they are accompanied and explained with words derived from science and theology. This does not leave the text dry or strung out, however. By no means. By doing so, we, the readers, excitedly follow his train of thought as he explores various ways to live life and deal with its challenges.

At times, Paul's writing is poetic and like experiencing a vivid dream or a French movie. He looks back on deep suffering and numerous near-death experiences from a perspective of gratitude and safety. But even more than gratitude and safety, there is a vivid liveliness to his reflections in both the telling and the reflections that come from his current mindset of spiritual liveliness. Paul writes for everyone, but with a special hope to connect with people who are currently in the same misery and confusion that he describes himself as having experienced. His story is an act of trying to knit together a fragmented experience of himself under the present self, which is one that is whole.

He describes a series of intellectual questions and conundrums that eventually become an intellectual pathway toward greater knowledge and openness of spirit. The stereotypically atheist fetishization of Society with a capital 'S' gives way to a meeting with the Man of Galilee in the community of believers in His Divinity. Intellectual issues with religion generally, and Catholicism specifically, are revealed to be motivated by deep childhood hurt and feelings of betrayal by both his dad and his community. He becomes motivated to win and outdo his father while avoiding the weakness of his mother at any cost. Religion, at first, is seen as something that weak people, like his mother, do. So, in his adolescence he avoids all religion and is given to railing against it as a complex method of social control. He outdoes his "atheistic biker dude" father by becoming an atheist graduate student in biology.

Instead of finding love and community as an atheist scientist, he becomes isolated and worn down. The struggle to survive eventually wears him down to the degree that his heart and mind open to Christians and to the Christian God. A beautiful trust-fund baby who is into the occult becomes like poison to his spirit, and eventually he finds that the way of his suffering mother is stronger than the way of his abusive, monstrous father. He turns from wasting away at the feet of this wiccan femme fatale to eating milk and cookies at the back of a Church of Christ in New Jersey.

He progresses from what he comes to consider a childish form of religious community to the more adult, rigorous and mystifying religion of his mother, Catholicism. He finally finds joy and strength in community that is focused around a divine person who is the embodiment of a single deity.

And he returns, eventually, to the Catholic Church, the church of his mother that deeply informed his sentiments and preserved him from the series of abusers on the model of his father that litter the first half of his life. What is particularly interesting to this editor about this text is that Paul does not complete his memoirs after his return to Catholicism. He minimizes describing his life as a Catholic living again in the community of Catholics; instead Paul focuses on trying to evangelize souls to know God.

To give away the ending, this return to the church of Catholic believers preceded Paul's marriage, having six children and the launch of a both successful consulting firm as well as a successful wealth management company. He writes looking back with gratitude for the current joy and abundance in his life. But, given the somewhat odd context of Paul feeling uncertain of how it is, exactly, that he survived all that he has, there are several elements of his life that seem odd or incongruent without being fatalistic. For example, the irony that the place on earth that attracts the most guttural, animal, barbarous humans—Wall Street—is where Paul goes not before, but after, he rejoins the Catholic church, and he sticks it out there for his lightness of heart, joy and loving ways. But he also perseveres on Wall Street for over eight years, more than twice the average duration of Wall Street workers.

He leaves with all the success, both social and financial, that he may have wished that his father had had. Gone are the days of agony and world weariness, viewing himself as others may have, as a specimen in a culture doomed to die. Now he is living in this sort of vibrant, mystical uncertainty where his basic longings and feelings about life have been extended beyond death into an afterlife. And to Paul has come the abundance of children and wealth and love and friendship. Like the biblical Job, the answer to his suffering isn't given here, though it is approached obliquely all throughout the text. No satisfying answer is given, as earthly promises are faulty, although there is much food for thought. But his awareness of there being room for goodness and innocence in the world that he and the reader live in may be the greatest gift of a book that appears to come full of gifts.

Lawrence R. Bilello III, Polyglot

Summary/Teaser

Warning to the hate-crime police: this memoir is not politically correct.

What it is, though, is a story very appropriate for Valentine's Day. It is a story of searching for truth and falling in love with something greater than oneself, greater than humanity, greater than nature, the world and the universe. Paul quickly realized - even as an atheist - that there is no point in trying to make everyone like you. No matter what position you take, there will always be someone on the opposite side of that opinion. Given that, we might as well pursue the truth and do what we think is right, correct?

Truth reveals itself as seen here in these three strange occurrences that challenged his concept of truth:

1. How does an atheist scientist end up married with several children? Is not the world overpopulating from the totalitarian perspective? If that is true, wouldn't having several children be irresponsible? Why would a trained doctoral scientist from a top university do such a thing? Was he not shocked when he found scientists, business leaders, doctors, scientists, engineers and other intelligent rational professionals were having more than two children?

2. How does a Wall Street analyst in New York City, often considered the center and top of the world, voluntarily leave Wall Street when there was more and more money to be made? Had he lost his marbles? What could be better than making a ton of money? But

then we look around and see that most Wall Street professionals do leave Wall Street on average about four years after starting... so the fact that Paul lasted twice that time also seems unlikely.

3. Why would a nerdy science geek break up with a handsome woman who comes from wealth? As an atheist, why would it matter that she claimed to be a witch? If there was no such thing as a witch, or anything like that, why care about any label she gave herself? Except ... was there trouble coming from being with a person claiming to be a witch?

Introduction

In 2016, I had the pleasure of being interviewed by Marcus Grodi on *The Journey Home,* a program on EWTN that shares the conversion stories of individuals who have come home to the Catholic Church. How I ended up on that program was a mysterious series of events. During my time as a Wall Street Analyst, an (heretofore) unnamed investment bank demanded I attend an Atlanta, Georgia conference at the last minute. All hotels in Atlanta, Georgia were already booked and the nearest flights and hotel they could find were in Birmingham, Alabama.

"Yeah, Paul. We rented you a Jeep and you can drive from Birmingham, Alabama to Atlanta, Georgia each day and come back each night." Well, I guess from New York City, all those Southern towns seem close together and drivable, but the actual distance was 150 miles through foothills and mountain ridges.

I was thinking about daring to say "no" to the 'big' investment banker when I was called by the president of the bank who said that they had changed their minds about my needing to attend the conference. I let the travel agency know, but they said the tickets were nonrefundable. So, I went back to my boss, the managing director of equity research, and asked if I could still use the tickets, hotel, car rental, etc. He said sure and then gave it all to me. Unfortunately, I was taxed as if it was a bonus the next year, but I did not find that out until later.

So, I called the travel agency and added my wife Mona and the three children we had at that time (two boys and a baby girl) to the flights and off we went on a week vacation with no pay and not a care in the world because we knew something. EWTN studios are in Irondale, Alabama, which is a quaint little suburb of Birmingham, Alabama. I called EWTN and arranged guest passes to the show tapings and we sat quietly in the audience watching Fr. Mitch Pacwa (a great guy, both on television and in person, who was baptized in Chicago), Raymond Arroyo, and Marcus Grodi. Marcus does not enter a room, he fills it! Marcus stands perhaps 6′10″ and weighs about 275 pounds, but you would never know that because he's always sitting during the show. Marcus also runs a 150-acre farm in Ohio which he revealed in his recent story, "Living on the Land."

After *The Journey Home* taping, we met Marcus. I should say we looked up at him, as the tippy-top hair on my head barely reached the sternum on his chest. I asked him how guests are selected. Marcus said people mail or email in their written faith testimonial/journey and his staff at the Coming Home Network in Ohio picks the guests. He also said not to have expectations of ever appearing on the show because they have a long list of scheduled guests and many, many testimonials mailed in each day that they screen meticulously. So, with no expectations, I wrote my story. At that time, it was mostly for myself, for the catharsis and self-retrospective inner-faith growth. Well, about 10 years later in 2015, I received an email that they wanted me as a guest.

At first, I did not want to go on *The Journey Home* show because it became a real possibility instead of a fantasy that was out of reach. My wife also had concerns that my being on international television would invade the privacy of our family. I told my spiritual advisor - a priest - that I did not wish to go. "But if your episode leads to even one conversion—" he began, and I finished his sentence "—I must do it." And he was right.

The night before the taping, I trembled. I was concerned about over-focusing on myself. I was also concerned that I should avoid naming anyone or any place identifiable that would harm anyone. At the same time, there were certain antagonists to my conversion I had to mention for the story to make sense. A deacon advisor emailed a reply to me in my darkest hour that night. His words gave me comfort, a path to follow: "Focus on each event and your internal response to only those events that led to your conversion." It was just what I needed to hear to avoid navel gazing, and I fell into a deep sleep. The next morning, I awoke late and had to rush-dress to be driven to a local parish for Mass. It was a brief daily Mass. Afterwards, the priest hugged me, thanked me for bearing witness, and gave me a blessing. I never caught his name, but I was grateful.

On that program, I shared part of the story of my difficult childhood, my rejection of the Catholic faith as a teenager, and my challenging years as an atheist in which I was searching for what was missing in my life. I just didn't know what that something was until I found it many years later back home in the Catholic faith.

Ultimately, my hope in sharing this more complete telling of my story is that my siblings, friends, acquaintances, and anyone reading this will consider a mature conversion, a true coming home to Jesus which includes following his walk to Calvary; to Home, Sweet Rome; and the Universal Catholic Church.

The Turning Point

Little did I know then the significance of the name of the street I lived on near Northwestern University's technology building: "Noyes." I realized sometime later that I lived out the first part of the word saying "no" to God when I arrived as an atheist graduate student, and that I would then live out the second part of the word saying "yes" to God as a Catholic, only after leaving Evanston. The street name Noyes has two parts = "No," followed by "yes." (Noyes is also the name of one of the original NU faculty members.)

I was finishing up a Ph.D. in Biochemistry and had just published articles that had attracted attention. I was on my way to interview at a pharmaceutical company to be a regulatory writer. Raised Catholic, I had rejected my faith and declared myself an atheist at age 16. By this time in my life, all I wanted was to be prestigious, powerful, and professional and this interview was my ticket to that life.

I put on my best suit and got into my car to head to what I was certain was the open door I had been waiting for. But, on my way there, I hit a patch of black ice, spun around in the road, and crashed into a ditch. Although there were other drivers on the road, no one seemed to see me, and no one stopped to help.

As I stepped out of my car, I fell into the mud. When I stood up, I saw that my fine suit was covered in muck up to my waist. My dress shoes now looked like workman's boots; the mud covering them was so thick and claylike. I wandered around the site of the accident trying to understand how I had crashed when everyone else on the road seemed to be driving by unscathed.

I looked around and saw a farmhouse nearby. I walked up to it. A dog barked at me and the farmer stepped outside. I explained what had happened. His response? "God will bring help."

What? I didn't need God. I needed a tow truck and a way to get to my interview. When I began to get upset, he asked me to leave.

As I trudged back to my car, I saw a tow truck approach. How could that be? I had only been gone a couple minutes. No one had called for help. Nevertheless, the tow truck was there. They brought me to a local repair shop where the car was determined to be fine. I tried to clean the mud from both the car and myself as much as I could. I called the HR person at the pharmaceutical company and explained what had happened. He said it would be fine to reschedule, but I was stubborn and did not want to miss my big chance. I insisted on going through with the interview. I did not get the job, but what I did find was far more valuable.

Chapter 1
From Light into Darkness
1969 Upstate New York

There was bright white light and a soft hum, a cool surface and a warm touch. The warmth was all around me. It stretched me out and dropped me down.

Before this moment, I knew everything. Maybe more appropriately, I knew the One who knows everything, and by knowing Him, I knew everything. But that was gone. I had no memory of it other than that it was, but I did not know anymore what I had known forever.

Now, I was small and surrounded by warmth. A blanket covered my legs. Above me floated a spinning swirl, and then the swirls focused into a ring of oval shapes suspended in the air on strings. Above the shapes, strings came together in a plastic ring and an arm draped from the side above them.

There was noise in the distance. It was voices. I was safe. I was warm. That was all I knew. But, the glow of all I knew before was gone.

****

1971

The voices murmured and laughed to one another. I looked up at a dusty ceiling with cobwebs. Plaster chunks hung from the walls. The older ones knew I was here, but they did not check. They continued. I hungered. I thirsted. No one checked.

The door handle was hanging, and the door lock broken. I dogged bags of mothball bags of old clothes and musty pulp novels in the hallway to the stairwell.

I stepped, I peeked, I walked down the steps until I saw them. My older brothers and sisters were laughing with one another, but they did not see me even now.

I ran down the stairs to the dining room and then to the kitchen. There were holes in the dining room ceiling and missing floor tiles on the kitchen floor. I slid an aluminum chair across the dusty floor, climbed the chair, opened the utensil drawer, stepped on the edges and onto the countertop, and reached into the cabinet to grab a brown jar. I got the knife, opened the fridge, and grabbed a loaf of bread. I opened the jar and used the knife to spread peanut butter on bread.

I put it in my mouth and chewed. I felt less hungry, but the peanut butter was too thick. I gagged, almost choked. I cried, shaking, squeezing the bread hard. I looked around, but no one was there. I could hear them, but they did not see me.

Alone. I was on my own at two years old.

****

I heard many voices, but where did they all come from? How many of us were there?

I looked at all my brothers and sisters. My youngest brother, 1; my three younger sisters, that made four; me, five; my three older brothers, eight; older sister, nine; older brother, ten, oldest sister, 11; oldest brother, 12. Wow, a dozen of us, like a dozen eggs, like *Cheaper by the Dozen* except that I was number eight, lost within the middle of a large family. Did they even notice I was here?

I bit stale crust. I slid a wet cloth down my legs, as urine drips down my shaking legs and pooled onto the floor. I wiped myself. I cleaned myself. I found clean underwear. I knew it was up to me to survive. I can do this, I think?

****

I was playing with a painted tin house. There were some open parts, cars, and figures of people. Some of the paint was chipping off and there were rusted corners, but it was beautiful.

I was pushed from behind. Crunch! It was no longer beautiful. There were drops of red on the house. My face and hands were in pain. What happened?

I smelled oil and steel. Big shoes were in front of me, walking away, down the stairs. Dad. It was him.

I ran down the stairs to the bathroom, crying, to put a cloth on my face. *Oh no, Dad's coming back.* Smack! My face was numb. My tooth fell out and more blood escaped onto my neck and shirt. There was such pain. Why?

I had to escape. I ran to my room and buried my face in my pillow before he could see me again. I watched as the red of my blood left dark stains on my pillowcase.

After a long while, my mom came to me and cleaned me up. She had such soft hands. I loved her smile and the sweet songs she sang to soothe me. She wrapped me in a warm towel and hugged me. I was safe in her arms.

****

My younger sister and I were watching Bugs Bunny in the living room. We could hear my parents' whispers from their bedroom next door.

"He is evil," I heard.

"No, he is not," Mom replied. My ears perked up. Who were they talking about?

"Paul is a bad boy!" Dad yelled. My heart sank with sadness and raged with anger.

"Shush!" Mom said.

"I tell you, he is bad."

I turned to my younger sister Esther. She turned to me.

"I'm going to kill dad," she said.

"No," I replied. "I should be the one to do it."

We both stared at the crack in the open door to our parents' bedroom. The voices were getting louder. Another fight, except this time it was about me. We cringed, stayed still, did not move. We covered our ears and hoped it went away, but we still heard them fight.

Kill dad. I couldn't let go of that thought. Did that mean he was right? Was I evil? I pictured picking up a knife from the kitchen. It was nighttime. I sneaked into their bedroom and stabbed him, again and again. He lay still. Now, he couldn't hurt us anymore. No, it was wrong. I couldn't do it. Something stopped me. I loved Mom. She would cry. I even … I even loved Dad.

I ran to the door, opened it, and ran up to Mom and Dad and hugged them.

"What do you want?!" Dad yelled.

"Frank!" my mom yelled back to him.

"Get out of here!" my dad yelled and pushed me back onto the floor.

My knees slowed me down as I grabbed for the rug with my hands, trying to escape. My knees burned in pain. I shivered. Rug burn again. I'd have to wear long pants again to school, to cover it up.

****

"A shining maze," I said.

"What's that, Paul?" my older sister Judith asked.

I grabbed her hand. "Come here! I'll show you."

I pulled her to the backyard. By the back fence next to the hanging laundry on the clothes hanger, between the hanging string and the evergreen tree, there was a fine gossamer net.

"Oh," said Judith, "a spider web!"

"Spider web," I said.

I stared at the web, it glistened in the sun. Dew drops outlined a large regular shape. I leaned in towards the spider.

I jumped up and down. "Look in there." I pointed to the middle.

"Oh yes, a spider," she said.

"Spider," I repeated.

The spider was brown with green on its back. The two front legs were longer than the other legs.

"What does it do?" I asked.

"Watch!" Judith picked up an ant and tossed it into the spider web.

The ant got caught in the web and wriggled and wiggled. The spider ran to the ant and started wrapping it up faster and faster in a spool of fine thread coming out of its behind.

"The web catches insects, and then the spider eats them," she explained.

I backed away, "Will the spider eat me?"

"No!" she laughed.

"What happens to the insects?" I asked.

"They die," she explained.

"Die? Forever?"

"Well, yes, but they kind of live on as part of the spider."

I placed my hands on my chest, curling up my fingers.

"Will I die?" I asked.

"Yes..."

I started to cry

"... and no. The soul lives on forever," she added quickly.

"Oh," I said.

Suddenly Judith's eyes grew as she looked up behind me.

I heard boots walking fast in the grass now. Judith fled. It was him. I wanted to run but couldn't.

"I kicked the dog all I could. Now I need something else - Paul, what are you doing back here?"

I cowered down. Dad glanced around at the clothes line.

"Oh, so you are knocking the clothes off the clothes line?"

"No," I said.

Dad took off his belt. "Come here."

I walked slowly towards him.

"Bend over!"

I did.

Smack, sting! Smack, sting! Smack sting! Seventeen times more...

I fell to the ground, panting...

"Wow, Paul," Judith said after it was over. "You didn't even cry."

"No need," I said rubbing my back side. "Even if Dad

kills me, my soul will live, right?"

"Yes," said Judith, and she helped me up.

I remembered Dad's smile as he came at me. He even smiled when he struck me. When he smiled, I saw his teeth. That must be the symbol of pain, teeth that want to eat me, teeth that want to chew on my bones, wanting to swallow me like the spider did to the ant. But, even if so, my soul will live on.

****

"Welcome, class," the kindergarten teacher smiled.

I saw her gleaming white teeth, reflecting the classroom fluorescent lights. I covered my eyes, but the tears came anyway. I wailed, I cried, I opened my eyes, I cried again.

The teacher was in front of me. "What is wrong?"

I cried louder, seeing her teeth so close to me. She stared at me, puzzled, and closed her mouth. I stopped crying.

The teacher opened her mouth again, "Now, class…"

I cried again.

The principal held my hand. Mr. Ritsome asked, "What is wrong, Paul?"

I cried. I went with him to the nurse's office.

The nurse tried to comfort me. "Now, everything is okay." I saw her pearly whites.

I cried more. The principal and the nurse exchanged glances. The nurse touched my knees with her hands. I recoiled as the rug burn under my pants stung. The nurse touched my arms. There were bruises under my shirt.

"Ow!" I said.

The principal stood behind me. "If you keep this up,

we will have to call your parents."

Oh no, I thought. I closed my eyes. That would be so much worse. I forced the tears to stop.

****

"Here is my bedroom," said my friend Timmy.

His room was full of bright toys and glowing colors. The rug whooshed between my toes. His bed had a comforter with a picture of *Star Wars* on it. His pillow matched his bed covers.

Wow, I thought.

"Let's play a game," Timmy said.

"Okay," I replied.

"Put your hands out like this," Timmy put his hands out flat in front of me. His nails and fingers were pink and perfect.

I did the same. My nails were too long, and dirt was under my fingernails and on my hands. He looked at my hands and then back at me. I pulled my hands away.

Timmy smiled. I cringed. He paused.

"You can use my bathroom to change into your pajamas," he said.

Pajamas? "Oh, uh, you go first?"

"Okay." Timmy went into the bathroom. I heard him call to me through the door. "Let's stay up all night! Do you want to play with my Lego sets or play *Go Fish* tonight?"

"What? Go fishing at night? Oh, no, I'm kind of tired. Maybe we can go fishing tomorrow?"

"Ha! Ha! Yeah, right!" Timmy was in a top and bottom that matched. The cloth looked like cotton. There were pictures of *Star Wars'* characters on his clothes like his bed sheets.

"Ha…" I fake-laughed.

"Okay, your turn." Timmy pointed to the bathroom.

"Oh," I thought fast. "Um, I … I forgot mine?"

"Oh." Timmy called, "Mom?"

"Yes, dear?" his mom peaked around the corner as if she were nearby the whole time.

"Paul forgot his pjs!" Timmy said.

"No problem," she said, "he can borrow your Lego pair. I just washed them. She reached into Timmy's middle dresser door and pulled out a top and bottom covered in Lego drawings.

"Oh!" I said, "Thanks." She handed me the clothes. I went into the bathroom and took off my hand-me-down jeans slowly trying not to sting my latest set of rug burns. I took off my oversized plaid shirt carefully avoiding my latest set of bruises.

I picked up the Lego bottoms and smelled them. They smelled like plastic wrap at a clothing store. I slid into them. The insides were smooth and did not rub against my shame wounds. The outside was soft but a little fluffy, just enough to notice. I yawned; they made me sleepy, safe and snug. I yawned again, and then I opened the bathroom door.

"Pillow fight!" Timmy threw two pillows at me at the same time.

"Yay!" I shouted, picking up two square pillows near the bottom of the bed and tossed them at Timmy's face.

He grabbed a few more pillows: one shaped kind of as a hexagon like starfighters and long thin ones shaped like lightsabers. He threw a few more. Where were all these pillows coming from? Did he grab all the pillows from the house and bring them here while I was in the bathroom?

"Ha! Ha! Got you!" He hit me in the tummy with the lightsaber pillow.

I doubled over in fake pain, "Ugh!" No, all these pillows matched his *Star Wars* and Lego sets. All these pillows? All these pillows were his.

"Come on!" Timmy said. "Let's get to bed." Timmy took the inside and I took the outside.

"Would you like the nightlight on in case you need to go to the bathroom?" his mother said.

"Nightlight?" I asked.

"Yes," said Timmy.

She turned on a little R2-D2 that was plugged into an outlet. Light came through and around the little plastic toy.

"Goodnight, boys," his mother said.

"Goodnight, Mom!" Timmy said.

"Goodnight," I whispered, still looking at the glowing R2-D2. I had never seen anything like, well, anything in this magical room! The light coming around the toy made the outline of the desk, dresser and bathroom door glow warm. I started to cry.

"What's wrong?" Timmy said.

I cried, I could not stop.

"What is it?!" Timmy shouted, shaking me.

I kept crying. I did not know such wonderful and beautiful things existed in the world. Sniff. Pajamas! Sniff. There was good in the world.

"What is it?" Timmy said.

Bed sheets! Sniff.

"Stop," Timmy put his fingers in his ears.

Shaped pillows. Sniff. Lighted toys. Sniff. Inhale. Sigh. Finally, I started to drift off to sleep.

Maybe life *was* worth living?

****

Smooth, thick, black cloth put on one sleeve, then on the other arm. Underneath there was crisp white, starched a bit, and tucked into dark slacks. A comb ran through my hair. I stood in front of a mirror.

"What a handsome little man!" Mom exclaimed, staring at my reflection in the mirror.

A little penguin of a boy looked back at me with dark shoes, dark pants, white shirt, and a dark sports coat. There was combed hair on a pumpkin head, big brown eyes, shifting right and left, and up and down.

"Another funeral?" I asked, remembering the hard, cool skin when I touched my great aunt's remains.

"St. Martha's School!" said Mom.

My eyes grew big. My fingers shook a little bit. I felt the urge to pee. Hairs on my neck stood up on their ends. Mom ushered me into the car. We drove the highway past the gorge and river, then stopped in a parking lot. There was a small orange bus. Penguins with backpacks and flower-dressed mops were hobbling out of cars to the bus. I followed.

High-pitched chatter, the smell of leather; I sat near the back alone. The seat bounced up and down along the road. The bus stopped in a blacktop parking lot. Across the street I saw St. Martha's Church.

We marched from the bus and towards a red-brick building. The brick looked like shiny sandpaper in the morning sunlight. Inside, we reached a classroom. The wood floors were waxed. Each desk was clean. The room smelled like lemon dish soap.

"Take your seat where your name is," a woman in a black dress and hood pointed to a chair. I searched until I found my name, "Paul." I sat there.

Everyone stood up, hand on chest, facing flag in front of room. "I pledge allegiance…" I went to sit down again. "Our Father, who art in Heaven…" I stood up again; everyone else was already halfway through the prayer when I joined in.

"Take your calendar book out of your desks," the nun began.

Next, we were on a black pavement play area. The boys were running around like chess players in little suits. The girls were spinning around, their dresses taut to their sides, like umbrellas. They looked like the flowers of the fields, so beautiful. The image snapped permanently into my mind, locked forever, so much light, so much joy, and then it was gone.

I was back on the bus, bumping along the road. I needed to pee. My hips, stomach and inside pants grew warm with yellow. My hands shook. I hobbled off the bus.

"Oh, this will never do," Mom picked me up and brought me to the car.

'Never' was right, for I never returned to St. Martha's Catholic School. The flicker of light went out as I fell back into darkness. *Why? Why show me such beauty, only to snap it away?*

Chapter 2
Back into the Darkness
1973

I was at the edge of the road and was about to walk up the sidewalk towards my friend David's house.

"Wait there!" said his father, quickly opening the window and giving me the stop signal with his hand.

"Here?" I looked around. "Yes, wait right there! I'll call David and he will come out to you." He motioned his hands slowly as if I did not understand.

I stood still, very still. A crow cawed in a nearby cornfield. David came to the front entrance and opened his front door. I waved. His dad grabbed his shoulder and whispered into his ear.

"Okay, Dad," David said, lowering his chin.

David walked to me but placed his right index finger in front of his mouth, motioning for me to keep quiet. I stayed very still until he reached the road.

"Come on," he said, looking back to his house as we walked to the playground.

"What was that about?" I asked.

"You cannot come to my front door."

"Why not?"

David was silent.

"Why?" I asked again, pulling on his arm.

"Your family, you are ... Catholics," David said, frowning and bunching up his shoulders when he said the word "Catholics" as if he just said a swear word.

"What does that mean?" I asked.

Rob threw him a basketball and we started playing.

"I have to go now," David said.

"What, you just got here?" I pleaded.

"Fifteen minutes, that is all we can play together," David said, turning his back to me, "and do not tell anyone we were together." He ran towards his house.

Really? I couldn't believe it.

"Paul, catch!" Rob said, throwing the ball at the back of my head. It bounced off the top of my head. He started laughing. Some friends. I put my hands in my pockets and walked home.

"Back so soon?" my mom asked.

"Yeah..." my voice trailed off as I sat at the kitchen table. "David cannot play with me much and I cannot go to his house."

"They're Southern Baptists," Mom said, plopping down instant potatoes on my plate. "When we first moved here, and they found out we are Catholic, we got a lot of angry phone calls."

"Like what?" I asked, spooning a piece of potato mush.

"You are going to burn in hell! The pope is the antichrist." Mom poured me some Kool Aid.

I gasped.

"It is not true," Mom said.

"Speak for yourself!" Dad hollered from the living room. "The Catholic Church is weak and you Catholics are inferior."

Mom shook her head, bit down on her teeth, and raised her spatula, as if Dad were a pesky fly she was about to swat. Then she calmed herself and plopped down canned peas next to my potato pile.

I watched Mom and wondered why she would believe in something weak and inferior?

****

"Yuck," Martha whispered to another girl, "he is one of that family of twelve kids!"

"How irresponsible," her friend said back.

What? So, I am irresponsible for existing?

Despite her words, I could not turn away from staring at her perfectly round face. Martha lifted her nose and walked away.

Oh well, I thought, *I guess even the girls not in my grade are aware of my family*. I asked my mom more that weekend.

"Why don't they like us? Is it just because there are twelve of us kids and we are Catholic?"

Mom answered, "I challenged one neighbor to tell me which of our kids should not exist and she just walked away."

"Wow. That's it?"

"No, not just that," Mom said, pausing to sip her tea. "Your oldest brother Daryl was salutatorian of his class—"

"Sol - Oh -Ta -Tor - Ean?" I said.

"Yes, he had the second highest grades in his class," Mom explained.

"And your oldest sister Pam was valedictorian of her class—she had the highest grades in her class."

"So?" I shrugged my shoulders.

"So, the town was not happy about that, and they changed the rules to include sports and extracurricular activities to become first or second in the class and to deliver speeches at graduation."

I thought about this all weekend. So, we believed weak ideas that were inferior yet had grades that were near, and at, the top? And that made people not like us? I didn't know what to make of that.

****

Something hard struck my back. Pain!

As I turned around to look, I heard the "whhhhrrr whack" as Malcolm hit me with another stone. This one struck my knee cap and made a "pop" sound.

I fell to the ground. *Not this again.* I was just walking down the street. Why was this happening? Malcolm ran to me with a wire cord in his hands, gleefully giggling as he tried to circle my neck with the wire. I blocked his strangle using my elbows to tangle up the wire, but I fell backward from the force of his blow.

Dirt covered my rug-burned forearms. I could see red bubbles percolating up from my wounds as I sat up, but wounds like this were nothing new to me.

Quickly, I spun around behind Malcolm and put him in a half-nelson. He spat the dirt from my left forearm and elbowed me in the chest.

"Pheew," my breath exited my mouth and nose.

I flipped him onto the ground in front of me, foaming at my nostrils.

Just as suddenly, my arms were bent behind my back and lifted upwards, forcing me to lean backwards but walk straight ahead.

"You rotten little brat!" I heard my father's charged voice whisper into my ear from behind.

I watched from my peripheral vision as Malcolm laughed and slinked away down the dirt road. Once I reached the yard of our house, I was thrown against the front steps onto the side of my body.

Smack! My elbow; Smack! My hip; Smack! My knee,

as I struck the concrete steps in succession down my side. Not exactly the sound of ringing church bells.

"You ..."

Whack!

How did he get his belt off so fast?

"worthless..."

Whack!

"son-of-a-"

"You! I'm a son of you!" I yelled, cringing in preparation for the next blow.

Kick!

"Shut up!" he yelled.

I fell over sideways.

Whack!

The belt again, this time it tore through my shirt and gashed my side and ribs.

It stopped?

I froze.

He leaned down to me. I could smell steel, oil and bad breath.

"You should never have been born," Dad whispered.

He dragged his belt up the front stairs and disappeared into the house.

I lay still, but then the shakes started. I knew this part, too, and was getting used to it. I did not bother to cry, instead, I just sat there.

I guess Dad agreed with my classmates at school.

Why was I alive? Neglected, then beaten, abandoned and betrayed, charged without a trial and accused without a jury, I questioned the value of my life. Was a life like *this* worth living?

Chapter 3
Escape into Imagination
1977

I picked myself up and dragged myself through the front door and into the bathroom. I wet a washcloth and bar of soap and rubbed the soap into the washcloth until it was soaped up and foamy. Then I rubbed the rug burns and the lashes, even though it stung. From experience, I knew it was best to clean the wounds right away.

I shed my dirty, bloodied clothes into the laundry basket and jumped into the shower. I ran the water until it was lukewarm and turned the knob for the shower.

Sting, sting, sting! There was stinging pain everywhere on my arms, back, side, knees, and shins.

I did not let the pain stop me. I rubbed each part clean until the red of my blood and the transparent water drained pink down at my feet.

I grabbed the reddish-pink worn-out towel and rubbed the clean skin hard. Then, I carefully pampered the areas where there were wounds, allowing the blood to absorb into the towel. After a minute, my breathing slowed but I started to feel the shakes again.

I wrapped myself in the towel and ran out of the bathroom and up the stairs to my bedroom. There, I found clean underwear, t-shirt, socks and baggy oversized pants. I put them on and fell into my bed.

I shivered, closed my eyes and slept in the middle of the afternoon.

I dreamed of a little man running out of the mouse

hole of our kitchen cabinet.

"Who are you?" I asked him.

"I'm Jimmie," the miniature person said.

"Jimmie?" I asked.

"Yes, Paul," the diminutive person replied. "I'm your imaginary friend."

"You are so little!" I said, laughing.

"So are you," said Jimmie, "for a person anyway."

"Well, what would you like to play?" I said.

"Anything you like." He moved away from me and started to run. "Catch me, if you can!"

I ran after him, up hills, down a creek, up a taller hill, on top of a cloud, into the sky?

"Where are we going?" I asked, wide-eyed as I peered down at the shrinking houses and trees.

"To show you beyond..."

"Beyond what?" I asked.

"To both the places that are bigger, and those that are smaller, than your world and all the places you can hide," Jimmie smiled.

I woke up. My eyes were big and stared at a small hole in the lower corner of the wall of my room.

"Jimmie," I smiled. "Where are you?"

Nothing happened, but then something moved in the corner of the hole.

"I'm here," said a little voice coming from somewhere down within the hole, "whenever you need me."

Maybe I could have another life—the one inside my head.

****

I was playing Candy Land with my brothers and sisters.

"Roll," said Alex.

I stared at the colorful board.

"It's your turn, Paul!" said Melissa.

"Oh," I picked up the white dice with black dots and rolled. I counted the spots.

"Come on," said Michael, "move already!"

I did. "One, two, three," I said as I moved my green gingerbread man three chits on the board. I jumped up and down in my seat.

"Great, yippee, you moved," Alex mocked my movements.

Michael waved his arm above my head, threatening to hit me. I ducked down and crunched my body into a ball. I did not care what my dad or brothers and sisters or classmates thought or did anymore. I crunched my body flatter.

"Push me down there," I said to Jimmie. My miniature friend flattened me and then slid me inside the board game…

Suddenly I was very small in a frothy confection. I was the green gingerbread man. Around me were colorful gumdrop trees as I crunched my cookie feet on candy cane grasses. The world of this candy land shone with colors brighter than reality.

Chomp. I bit down on a chocolate board of a small home.

"Mmm," I said.

"Mmm, what?" Alex asked me.

"Mmm … tastes good," I replied slowly.

"You lost, Paul, since you just sat there, duh'ing, when it was your turn," said Melissa.

"Yeah, doofaas!" Michael folded up the board and

placed it in the game box. "Game over!"

I did not reply. Instead, I closed my eyes.

"What are you doing? Melissa asked.

"I do not need the board anymore," I replied.

I could barely see or hear as Melissa and Alex looked at each other and then shook their heads and walked away.

Then, I was back in the candy land.

"Let's play!" Jimmie exclaimed.

"You're too big," I said, "but I can fix that." I blinked my eyes and Jimmie and I were both now gingerbread men on the candy path.

"I'm hungry," Jimmie said. "I want some marshmallows."

"I can fix that," I replied. I waved my cookie arms and an army of little marshmallow men appeared in front of us.

When they saw us lick our lips, the marshmallow men exchanged glances and started to flee. We gave chase with plates in one hand and hammers in the other.

An imaginary life. Now *that* was a life full of candy and fun.

****

My agnostic older brother Michael introduced me to *Dungeons & Dragons*. From there, I fell into the well of playing other role-playing games. I lived in alternative realities where I had the ability to make up the rules and influence the outcomes. I delved further and further from reality. Also, from reading science fiction,

I began to understand the unsaid rules of world creation.

Ice hung from the roof. The walls were cold. The sun hung low. The winter was deep, and I led my younger brother Matt to play.

"Strength, Intelligence, Dexterity, Wisdom, Constitution and Charisma."

Matt scribbled the first two words on a blank piece of paper and then paused. "Slow down. I can't write that fast."

I yawned, tossing one of Mel's throwing stars at a crayon drawing of a life-size giant on the bedroom wall. Another big chunk of plaster fell onto the floor in a poof of dust. Two by fours and wooden slats were exposed and resembling the bars of a prison. "You can abbreviate the primary characteristics as STR, INT, DEX, WIS, CON, and CHA," I said.

"I thought that was for *Dungeons and Dragons*?" Matt asked.

"Pretty much the same characteristics in Mutant World."

"Mutant World?" Matt asked.

"Yeah, it is my latest creation. Just write it down." I said.

Matt wrote down these mysterious abbreviations. "I thought role-playing was supposed to be a fun game!"

"It is," I told Matt.

"Then, why do I have to write all this stuff down? It feels like school."

"You're making a character. The more you write about him, the more realistic he becomes. It's fun, you'll see."

I had found a 'reality exit.' If I could not make it in the real world, then I could make it in an imaginary world. Jimmie started it, or, that is, the Jimmie of my imagination. I did not start it, but I planned to explore the limitless landscape of my own imagination. Three hours of dice rolling, and chart consulting gave Matt six characters and an aching headache.

"Can we have some real fun now? I want to kill that jerk, Yacorn." Matt pounded his left palm with his right fist.

"It won't be easy. He's on a quest for the first hundred worlds."

"What's that?" Matt asked.

"Every generation, three adventurers compete to become King of the First Hundred Worlds. One will be good ..."

"That's me!" Matt drummed on his pigeon chest.

"No, you're not good. You killed imaginary people, remember?"

"Oh, yes, so I did. Then, who represents good?" Matt asked.

"Davron did, until Yacorn tricked you into blowing him up," I said.

"That jerk! When I get my hands on him, I'll—"

"—There'll be plenty of time for revenge. You represent neutrality. That means the group of people who are neither good nor evil, but who stand up for themselves."

"Makes sense. You don't have to tell me who represents evil. I'll crush Yacorn's head and ... " Matt crumpled a piece of paper into a ball.

"Hey, that's your character sheet for Vanslay!" I pulled the crumpled sheet out of Matt's hand and flattened it with his hand on the desk.

"Sorry. I didn't kill him, did I?"

"The paper merely represents Vanslay. He's fine."

"So, when do I get to kill Yacorn?" Matt asked, wide-eyed.

"With God sword, but first you have to represent neutrality. After killing innocent people, you must accomplish something good, or your balance will tip toward evil. If you become evil, Yacorn wins."

"I'll kill Yacorn with God sword serve good," Matt concluded.

"No, murder is not good. A good person, like Davron, would try to place Yacorn in jail by finding evidence against him."

"That's boring. What does neutral do to win?" Matt asked.

I replied, "The traditional way for a neutral contestant to win is to be the first to explore all one hundred worlds. If you reach the 100th world first, with the help of God sword, then you rule them."

I do not know if God sword came from faith. I think it was just a neutral weapon Matt could summon for help. Perhaps this lived out my desire for a benevolent protector in the form of justice. Except this protector was just a sword, not God, and a weapon that did whatever Matt wanted when he needed it most, so was not really justice either.

Matt imprisoned many bad opponents on adventures throughout my imaginary universe. I then lived vicariously through my younger brother, who I let win every sport and master every area of human life that our imaginations could play out in our parents' home and hamlet.

I found the real world was rarely there for me. All I needed was food, clothing, a bathroom, and sleep. All the other times were just pain, but I kept going as my mind anticipated the good times in my imaginary universe to come.

In my imagination, Matt or I could have power, wealth and glory. All imaginary boys were my friends and all imaginary girls were my girlfriends. Natural law was mine to make and logic and rules were at my whim and fancy. Matt and I became our own gods, able to escape the reality that I did not make, understand, or fit into.

Yet, even in my imaginary world, I always ended with good triumphing over evil. Why did I do that when I had told Matt that he represented neutrality?

Chapter 4
Dad Out, Mom In
1981

"I was never a Catholic!" Dad yelled.

Mom put her hand over her mouth and her eyes widened. "But you took an oath on the altar!"

"I lied," Dad said quietly.

"So, it was all just for show?" Mom put her arms at her sides.

"Not always. When Dad was alive, I was able to lean on his faith," Dad said.

"So, what, when Dad died, you just … just …" Mom fumbled for the words.

"There was no one to give me strength," Dad said, trying to hold Mom.

Mom sobbed, pushing his arms away, "Your faith cannot be based on another person's faith."

"Shush," Dad said.

His facial expression flattened as Dad realized he had an audience.

"There, there," Dad tried to pat Mom on the shoulder, but she pulled away. "It just kind of slipped away with time. Who really knows if there is a God anyway?"

By the last sentence, Mom was staring right at me. I froze.

"There's pasta in the kitchen," Mom said to me, rubbing my arm and turning me away from Dad's gaze and towards the kitchen. "Now, hurry up and eat so we can go to Mass."

"What's the point? The existence of a god is

anybody's guess. Just stay here and watch TV," Dad pointed to the living room. As he smiled, his teeth flashed, and I shivered from the memories of his beatings.

"No," I said softly and ran to the kitchen.

Dad was out, and Mom was in. I could always count on her. Mom loved me, comforted me, and fed me. What did Dad do other than harm me? Was that all a dad was for? Did he serve no purpose other than torment?

****

"Time to go to your First Holy Communion class!" Mom yelled up the stairs.

"I'll be right down!" I yelled. I sat in a desk two sizes too small for me, leaning forward writing with black pen on lined paper. I was nearly done creating the next adventure for Matt. *Damn, I'll have to get back to it later.* I ran down the staircase.

"What's the point in making them go to those CCD classes?" Dad leaned in toward Mom. "They are just going to stop going to church, when they are free."

I heard Dad and turned around to go back upstairs.

"Hush!" said Mom, waving Dad away. "Paul, you are going to your church class. Now, get dressed."

I glanced at Dad who was retreating to the living room. I grabbed my hand-me-down coat from the leaning coat rack, sat on the water radiator in the kitchen to warm up, put on my old shoes, and headed out to the car.

Mom turned the key in the ignition. "Whirr, whrrr-rrrrr ... kaplumnk!" went the engine failing to turn over. Below the rusted hood was a 1972 Buick Electra 6-

cylinder, struggling to stay alive.

Mom pressed down on the gas again.

"Don't flood her!" I said.

She turned the key again, grunted as the engine turned over, and we backed out of the dirt driveway. Dust came up around the car and a bit in the open windows, our version of air conditioning.

"I don't understand what's happening at the church class," I said to Mom.

"Just pay attention," she blurted, cranking the manual steering wheel around and around while she huffed and puffed as if she were Captain Hook manning a pirate ship.

Father Matt waved as we arrived at the front steps of St. Martha's Church.

The usual six kids were sitting in the front pew. I walked slowly up the aisle to the front row and sat. I folded my arms and leaning forward until my head touched the wood of the hand railing.

I counted to 100, then back down to 0, still no teacher.

I stared at my dirty hands, seeing the dirt under my fingernails and the dirt on my joints, and followed with my eyes the curves of skin folds that made up my fingerprints.

Fr. Matt must have given up on the teacher showing up as well. He came to the front of the church.

"Okay," he said, "let's see what you have learned, as we say: Hail Mary, full of grace…

"Hail Mary, full of grace…," we echoed back slowly.

"The Lord is with thee…"

"The Lord is with thee…" *What did that mean anyway? Was the Lord standing next to Mary? Was he like a coach in a football game?*

"Blessed art thou amongst women..."

"Blessed art thou amongst women..." *What was so special about her anyway? Was she blessed just because we say she is blessed or was there another reason?*

"And blessed is the fruit of thy womb, Jesus."

"And blessed is the fruit of thy womb, Jesus." *Does that mean Jesus is fruit? What is a womb? Is that like a wound?*

"Holy Mary, mother of God..."

"Holy Mary, mother of God..." *Wait, was she the mother of God the Father or Jesus the son?*

"Pray for us sinners..."

"Pray for us sinners..." *So, I knew we could pray for each other, but how did a dead lady pray for us*?

"Now, and at the hour of our death. Amen."

"Now, and at the hour of our death. Amen." *What about all the times between now and when I die? How will I know to pray when death approaches? How will I know what hour is my death?*

"Okay," Fr. Matt slapped his hands together. "Looks like we're all done here for today, so we'll see you next week for your First Holy Communion. Remember to either hold out your hand or stick out your tongue to receive Jesus." He smiled and walked away.

So, I had to *eat* Jesus? Cannibalism? *Eat* him, I barely even *knew* him! It just seemed like a big leap forward in my friendship with the guy. I wasn't sure I was ready for that, ... but if they said so, oh well.

The dust ball of our car spilled around the corner to the front steps. When the dust settled, I pulled open the 300-pound door, squeeeek. I got in and sat on the broken springs.

"So, Paul," Mom smiled, "are you still interested in

being a priest?"

"Well, priest or doctor," I replied, glad she was interested in me. "I figure, either I want to heal people's bodies or their souls."

Mom patted me on the leg, "Either one, both are good choices."

Chapter 5
No Religion, No Cry…Yet
1983

One day in high school, girls stopped being quite so annoying. It was a weird and sudden change.

Kara had feathered hair, red lipstick, blue eyeliner, pink blush, and she was smiling at me. I was hypnotized as if the Baptist minister's daughter were an exotic fish in the ocean. I could not peel my eyes away from her.

Kara held me close and pecked me on the cheek. "Hurry, follow me," she said, holding my hand and pulling on me. I followed willingly.

My friends had warned me not to date her, but I ignored them. After all, she was beautiful, and she had asked me out. She was a welcome distraction from the mess that was my life.

This was our third date and somehow, we were in front of the Southern Baptist church. She had sort of maneuvered me there.

It was a small chapel about the size of a one-room school house. We walked in holding hands. All eyes were on us, or so it felt. She sat me in the front row on a creaky wood bench. Her father was standing in front of us at the pulpit.

Rev. Lambert started preaching. "The Catholics worship idols!"

Maybe, I thought, whatever. Kara squeezed my hand.

"The pope is the antichrist!" he continued.

I raised my eyebrows. I no longer believed in the Catholic faith, but his words seemed extreme because I did not believe in a Christ or antichrist.

Rev. Lambert now stood right in front of me. He looked directly at me, "… and Catholics are going to hell!"

I turned to Kara and saw a question mark in her eyes. I was an atheist and I did not believe in a heaven or hell or anything supernatural, but somehow that conclusion really irked me.

I frowned at Kara and turned away from her father. At that moment she became my ex-girlfriend. I wondered how many other boys had been subjected to this…this routine?

I walked out of the church and never looked back. I felt embarrassed and insulted, even though I could not understand why I was offended. I decided that not only would I not be a Catholic, but I would also not be a Protestant because they tricked and trapped people.

Still, the fact that I had taken offense at anti-Catholic slams continued to trouble me.

I noticed another girl, Jeannie, walking down the hallway. She passed me, smiling, and I looked back at her. My eyes widened at what I saw: round girl magnets. My heart started beating hard.

Now my only thought was why I had not noticed this before. I glanced back at her again. She had stopped, hand on one hip, slightly lifting her dress above her calf, and turned to face me. She smiled. I smiled back.

She walked back and directly up to me, sort of swaying side to side like a seasick walrus, but I was hypnotized by every move she made.

"Hi, Paul," she said, still smiling, touching my hand.

My eyes grew round, my pupils froze, and my head tilted. "Hi."

Jeannie touched her hand on my shoulder. Even her little fingers were round and warm. "Bye," she said, strolling away again, this time very slowly, looking back at me staring at her the whole way down the hall.

Only when other kids blocked my view of her, and the hypnotic spell was broken did I realize she had handed me a folded-up piece of lined paper. I unfolded the paper nervously. It was notebook paper, the ripped frills still clung along one edge. Blue pen cursive handwriting covered the page. I ducked into the boys' restroom and closed a toilet stall. Then I read:

Dear Paul, I like you. Do you like me? I've noticed we see each other between class periods in the hall sometimes. I hope you like me. This is my second year at school here. I noticed you last year, but it took me a while to have the guts to write to you. Please be nice if you do not like me. And, if you like me … like I like you :), then call me. XOXO -Jeannie.

Someone likes me? Really like-likes me?

****

"Yeah…" I whispered on the phone, lying on the kitchen water-heater board.

"Paul, time to go!" Mom yelled up the stairs.

"Gotta go, Jeannie." I said. "I love you, too. Bye."

I walked from the kitchen to the dining room, where I stood behind Mom.

"Paauuuuul!" Mom still called up the stairs.

"I'm right here, Mom." I touched her shoulder from behind.

"Ah!" Mom held her chest and she sighed. "Were you on that phone with Jeannie again?"

I lowered my head.

"She's not for you, young man," She scolded. "Let's go."

We got into the jalopy and moseyed over to St. Martha's for my last Confirmation class.

"So," Mom smiled, "which one is it going to be, doctor or priest?"

I shook my head, still thinking about how many minutes I would need to wait to speak to Jeannie again.

In the front pew, my classmates were there flopping around awaiting our 'good' teacher who would never arrive during the class.

"Did you go to Jim's party?" Lucy asked David.

"Oh, yeah, I got hammered!" he replied.

"I heard you vomited in the toilet." Lucy folded her arms.

"Yeah, it was awesome," he said, laughing.

I shook my head and thought that either partiers were stupid, or I just did not have a life. I leaned toward my not having a life. With my friends partying and experimenting with drugs and sex, I wanted to join in the revelry.

"Here are my good students," said Fr. Tom. The class that never started was about to end again. Let me guess, another repeat-after-me prayer?

"Young men and women," Fr. Matt looked at us, "you are about to be confirmed, and once you're confirmed, you're an adult! So, then you can freely choose to go or not to go to Mass and to observe or not observe the faith."

What? I had a choice? I could just stop going? Then I could drink, do drugs and do stuff with a girl?

That Easter was my Confirmation. Mom made me

wear a suit that had belonged to one of my older brothers. She was so proud of me. I didn't want to let her down.

"The bishop will call you up shortly," Fr. Matt informed my classmates and me as we gathered at the entrance of the church. He walked away to shake the hand of a large white-haired man with a red beanie on his head, a staff at his side and long red robes that nearly covered his red shoes.

Organ music played. We all stood up. The bishop was at the altar and ushered us forward. We clumsily walked up to the altar, heads down, and stood in a line before the bishop.

He said prayers, spoke to us, raised his hands, and made the Sign of the Cross on our foreheads. I did not feel any different. All I wanted was to get to see my latest teen crush.

Mom and I got into the dust box and bumbled along the road all the way home.

"So," she said, "Priest? Doctor?" Mom smiled.

"Not a priest," I said, folding my arms. I pictured Father Matt's goofy smile and rambling talks. Who would want to be him?

"Oh, that's too bad." Mom really sounded down.

"Doctor," I said loudly, to cheer her up. "I will be a doctor."

Mom nodded and grinned. Her chapped lips showed through waxy red lipstick.

Once home, I reached for the kitchen phone, but Mom put her hand over mine and lowered the phone back onto the handle.

"Maybe take a break from Jeannie," she said.

That was it! I thought. *I want what I want, and I want it now*. So, I turned to Mom suddenly and blurted out, "Mom, I am no longer Catholic."

Mom and I stared at each other for a moment. I could see the pain in her face. I could not believe what I had just said, but I felt like I had to go through with it if I was to have what I wanted: Jeannie, parties, fun.

Mom hugged me, said "No!" and cried.

My dad patted me on the shoulder. Part of my decision was to get my father's approval. Part of it was that my friends were delving into pleasures, and I wanted to do that too. I also wanted acceptance. My friends were Protestants. I wanted to fit in with them. Why should I keep being Catholic? I knew nothing.

"Why, Paul?" Mom said. "Did I do something wrong?"

"Fr. Matt," I said. "You know, Fr. Cool Priest said, 'Once you are confirmed, you are an adult in the Church, and you can choose to be Catholic, or not be Catholic.'"

"Huh?" Mom said, scolding. "Don't speak about a priest like that!"

My mother had entrusted others to educate me, but I went to a public school where kids took drugs and teen girls got pregnant. Mom had entrusted others to form me, but Fr. Matt and his staff had taught me next to nothing about the faith.

"It doesn't matter, Mom. I choose not to be Catholic," I said. "That's all. It's no big deal." I glanced at her, "Mom?"

She was sobbing into a handkerchief.

"You are only 16 years old...what do you know?" She trembled. "What will happen to you?"

I tried to hold her, but she pushed me away.

I stared at Mom and Dad: her crying and him sneering. My parents fought a lot, likely due to their different beliefs. I saw no peace. I wanted peace. Neither belief appeared to promise peace.

Part of my rebellion was the thought that I would do something other than the two choices my parents provided. I decided to just be on my own. My dad had planted enough doubt in my mind that I decided if I was not Catholic, then I would just be an atheist.

"I'll be okay," I told Mom. "Now I can do as I like."

Was I trying to console her, or was I trying to console myself?

****

I watched my dad listening to my older sister.

"Then Sarah and Karen went to the mall..." Pam rattled on.

Dad stared at her, nodding and smiling. I shifted my seat from a chair to the radiator cover. Now I could see where he was looking—at her eyes. What was so special about her eyes? They were just blue marbles.

"...then we met Ken and I think he's going to get that job at Superfoods," Pam continued.

Huh? I thought. *It was just the ordinary events of her day.* Was that what fascinated Dad?

Beep! Beep! A blue Ford Bronco waited out front.

"Gotta go, Dad, Ken is here to pick me up," she stood and hugged dad.

"Have a good time," he said, hugging her.

"Bye," Pam said in a high lilting tone that trailed off and she left.

There must be a pattern to those who won Dad's approval, but what was it? Even my leaving the

Catholic faith hadn't seemed to make any difference. As far as Dad was concerned, I was still a loser.

Just then, my brother George skipped into the kitchen, snapping his fingers.

"Hey, George," said Dad, "do you have band practice tonight?"

"Yup," George said, clapping to an unseen beat.

Again, Dad looked right into his eyes. More blue marbles. What's with that?

"Do you have a ride?" Dad asked.

"Nope," George turned around.

Dad took out his keys, "Here you go."

George grabbed the keys and without a word, split.

So, I thought, *maybe if I just act casual, I will get my way?*

Dad finally saw me on the radiator. He frowned.

"So, today I spoke to Jeannie…" I started, leaning back.

"Shut up!" Dad shouted, looking to the left of me. Did he have trouble seeing me? I could not change my eye color to blue. There had to be another way to get his attention.

What do I do now? I tried acting casual. I clapped my hands together and tried to make eye contact.

"And stop that racket!" Dad screamed, red-faced, staring past me. "Now," Dad composed himself, "clean off the table and do the dishes."

"But it's George's night for kitchen duty…" I said, wondering if my eyes were hard for him to find.

"He's busy, get to it!" Dad raised his hand to strike me.

This time, I did not cower. Instead, I acted calm and lifted my chin.

He lowered his hand. Dad's eyes finally met mine. George called brown eyes like dad's and mine "poop-colored" eyes. Dad's poop eyes peered into my poop eyes. Correction, he peered up at me. The whites of his eyes grew for a moment, then shrank again. I realized I could see Dad's thinning hair at eye level. *Was I taller than Dad now?*

He walked out of the kitchen towards the living room. I realized I could see the top shelf of a cabinet above his head. *Taller,* I thought. *I am taller than him now.*

While I had failed to successfully imitate Princess Pam or Prince George, there was a slight victory here. For the first time, Dad had backed off instead of smacking me. He wanted to hit me but had not. Was Dad afraid of the taller me? He never struck me again.

****

"So, you think you are good at chess?" Dad leaned towards me, placing his black pieces on the board.

I did not speak, since I had learned that even imitating the words and gestures of the winners did not work with Dad. I just quietly set up the white pieces.

It was over in ten moves. I did not even utter the word, "Checkmate."

Smash! Dad knocked over the pieces.

I had won, just like I read about in *My 60 Memorable Games* by Bobby Fischer. Fischer had taught me to crush my opponents and to show no mercy. Attack, attack, attack. Find your opponent's weaknesses and destroy him without letting up.

I leered at Dad. He would not look me back in the eyes. *Coward,* I thought. Only winning, only strength mattered. Victory was mine.

"Dinnertime!" Mom screamed in a high-pitched trill. We came running from all directions.

"Bless us, oh Lord, and these thy gifts…"

"Blah, blah, blah," said Dad, adding, "Let's eat!" He picked up a piece of fatty steak and shoved it into his mouth.

I ran to the living room with my bowl, my three younger sisters behind me. The sound of chomp, chomp, chomp eating behind us.

"I just cannot eat in the same room with Dad," Cathleen sneered.

Scream. Jumping! "Blah! Ah!" Dad yelled.

I ran back to the kitchen. Dad had a purple head, the skin on his face was flush. He was jumping up and down and waving his arms. Was he choking?

I ran to him, went behind him, put my arms around his waist, and cupped my hands together. Then I quickly pulled towards me and upwards at the same time. One, two, three times. He spit out a piece of steak fat.

Dad huffed and puffed, catching his breath as his head went through various colors from purple to red to pink to tan again.

"You saved him!" Mom told me.

Why would I save him? I remembered my fantasies of stabbing him to death. I never acted on them, but those memories reminded me of the angry injustice I felt towards him. I could not move. Correction, why *did* I save Dad? It was as if it needed to be done, but why did

I do it? I could conjure up no emotional justification. *There must be some other reason,* I thought, but it was beyond my reach to understand at that time such natural law ideas as the intrinsic value of all life.

"No dish duty for one month," Dad proclaimed, pointing his arm into the air, the king of nothing.

Yeah, I thought, and walked back to the living room to watch the *Pink Panther* cartoon while eating from my plate, losing myself in the cartoon world.

Why did I save my tormentor? It made no sense. I wanted to be a winner. Don't winners crush their enemies, not save their lives? Did it matter that Dad still lived?

Chapter 6
Infatuations
1985

"Heart beats silly like a big bass drum." Rod Stewart's voice blared on the radio.

I combed my hair in the mirror, folding over the hairs to feather it.

"Losing all equilibrium," Rod continued.

I put on a tacky gold chain my mom bought for me.

"It's so hard in the middle of the week," sang Stewart.

I put on my Scott Baio Hawaiian shirt. Groovy.

"Maybe this woman's just all I need." Rod, now, bring it home.

I brushed my teeth to pearly white.

Knock! Knock! "Hurry up in there!" Michael yelled.

"Oh no, not again
It hurts so good
I don't understand
Infatuation
Infatuation
Infatuation
Infatuation
'Fatuate me, baby"

I stared in the mirror. I was ready to go.

I opened the door.

"Hmph," Michael said, slipping past me to enter the bathroom.

Mom eyed me up and down and smirked.

"All right, Paul," Mom said. "Get in the car."

I tried to act casual and jumped in the jalopy.

As we reached the movie theatre, Jeannie was already getting out of her mom's car.

When the theatre lights went out, we kissed. From there, well, basically, I had to re-watch the movie *Crocodile Dundee* because I have no memory of anything but her.

"Bye," she said, red-faced, jumping in her car after the show.

While it felt good to make out with her, as her mom's car drove away, I felt terrible.

Why should I feel terrible? I thought going to second base would make me feel good.

The next day we spoke on the phone at our usual afterschool time. She was sullen.

"What's wrong?" I asked.

"You were too aggressive," Jeannie said.

I paused, holding the phone. "Sorry," I shook my head. "I thought that was what you wanted."

"Why did you think that?" Jeannie asked.

"Because you said, 'I hope you will be bringing your "A" game?'" I explained.

"Yeah, I guess I should not have revved you up like that..."

"So, neither of us really wanted to do anything in the movie theatre?" I asked.

"I wanted to see the movie," she said.

"Me too," I replied.

We laughed.

But I did want her. Or, did I want her approval? What exactly did I want with her?

****

"Hey, Paul, we've got a job for you," James said as he, Mark, and Dave nodded and exchanged glances.

"We need you to make a pick-up. Here's thirty dollars," Dave said, handing me a ten and a twenty.

I stared at the bills. I'd never handled anything bigger than a one-dollar bill.

"Donald will meet you at the bridge with the booze," Mark said.

"Why me?" I asked.

James shrugged. "We would get into trouble, but your parents don't mind."

They don't? My dad's angry face came into my mind. No, they do mind, but I wanted to be liked by my friends. "Okay."

I made the pickup of a bottle of rum, then walked to James' house holding the paper bag by the neck of the bottle, terrified that someone would see me. I breathed a sigh of relief once his door closed behind me. I lifted the bag and handed it to James.

"Great," James said. "Now place it on the table." His eyes darted around nervously, then he pulled out three two-liter bottles of soda. He opened a cabinet and set out two rows of glasses on the tables and poured soda into them, filling each of the glasses half-way.

"We want it to be undetectable," he said.

"Sorry?" I asked.

"You're good at chemistry, right?" James asked.

"Yeah?" I said slowly.

"Great, so add the rum a little at a time to soda in

these glasses and find the undetectable amount."

"Titrate?" I asked.

"Yeah, sure, titrate, whatever. Just make sure no one can taste the rum."

I did what James wanted. I added a very small drop of rum to the first glass of soda. James drank it. He paused and then nodded.

I added about a half-tablespoon to the next glass of soda. Again, James drank, paused and nodded. I added a little more rum progressively to each glass until James shook his head side to side. I then reduced the amount of rum a tiny bit. James drank, paused, nodded, and gave me the thumbs up.

"This is it," James said, "the biggest dose that I still cannot taste. Good job." James started emptying the soda into the sink.

I helped him move the two unopened sodas into a camping cooler. I covered the rum with the brown paper bag and put that into the cooler as well.

"All set for the party," James said, rubbing his hands together.

"What party?" I asked.

James looked away. "Yeah, I guess you would need to mix the drinks…"

I was silent.

"Mark's lean-to party in the forest, tonight."

"Okay," I said.

"Yeah, be there before sunset," James said.

"And after that?" I asked.

"You can stick around if you like…" James showed me the door. "See you tonight."

The trail in the woods was overgrown with weeds. I looked down as I stepped on poison ivy. There was a striped yellow caterpillar on a milkweed. Normally, I would have stopped to watch it eat those thick green leaves as white liquid dripped out. But now the sun was lower in the sky, so I hurried along the trail to the lean-to.

"Hurry up," Mark yelled as I approached.

Mark, James, and Dave had already set up. The glasses were lined up on the cooler top, each half full of soda. Measuring spoons were on the paper bag next to the rum.

I mixed; they tested the drinks, giving the thumbs up.

I could hear the high-pitched rumble of girls walking down the trail behind me. Mark, James, and Dave rushed to make sure everyone had a drink in their hands. I turned around to see our guests. Yep, just as I thought, all girls. There was Sharon, Kathy, Stacey, and what? What were my sisters Cathleen and Melissa doing there?

"You, you … do not want that," I said to my sisters, pulling the glasses from their hands.

Their eyes shrank, but before they could protest, I poured Cathleen and Melissa glasses of straight soda.

"Here you go," I said, "these are fresh drinks."

I glared at James. He shrugged his shoulders.

As the shadows deepened, I tended the campfire, putting myself in a position to watch my sisters all evening.

"You can go home now," Mark said.

I nodded. I didn't want to be there anymore.

"Cathleen, Melissa, come with me," I said.

"What?" Cathleen replied.

"Why?" Melissa asked, "We're having a good time. Why are you trying to ruin our fun?"

"Mom said we had to be home before bedtime," I lied. Our parents rarely checked on us or set any curfews. They got up and followed me with folded arms and pouty lips.

I had known what the plan for the evening was, and I was okay going along with it to be liked by my friends. I also suspected girls were involved and was glad at first to hear them coming, but all that changed when I saw my sisters there. Why did that matter to me? As a cynical atheist, I should have been glad that my sisters would have had fun. After all, what was life about, if not having fun? But I was not happy.

The moral problem troubled me. Was I okay giving a "roofie" to strangers but not when they were given to my family? I also knew the other girls because they were my sisters' friends. I knew them and did not want to participate. That also posed a problem for me, for any stranger once you know them becomes a friend. Once a friend, I did not want to trick them, so why would I want to trick anyone, knowing they could be a friend? It was as if in theory, it sounded great, but in practice, it was deplorable. Why? I was silent all the way home.

****

"I went to Andrea's house," Daniel said, "and we had sex."

"Really?" I asked.

"Yeah, she said her parents were gone and I should come over," Daniel explained excitedly.

"Just like that?" I asked. Andrea always seemed to me

to be a little mentally unstable.

"It took maybe 15 minutes, is all," he said. "It was awesome."

I pictured them together, and then shook my head. He did the mental girl?

"What's wrong?" Daniel said.

"Nothing," I said, looking down, red-faced. Was this sex thing so great that taking advantage of a mentally unstable person was acceptable?

"Everybody's doing it!" he said, walking away.

I wasn't doing it. I did not feel ready, even though I wanted to. Was I required to have sex?

The memories of that conversion came back to me as I dipped my paint brush into thick red paint.

"How long have you been dating Jeannie?" Bob asked, turning on a fan towards the last strokes of wet paint.

"Six months, why?" I replied.

"And all you have done is kiss her and hold her?"

"Yeah," I whispered.

"Man," Bob shook his head. "If you do not get some action soon, that girl will move on!"

"Girls do not want that," I said weakly, not sure what I believed anymore. I thought of my sisters and mother, but what did I really know about what they wanted?

"Believe me, they do," Bob said. "And girls get bored if you do nothing."

"Huh?" I said. Jeannie had whispered in my ear, encouraging me, hugged and kissed me, but I had never seen her as the aggressor. I thought I was the aggressor and felt ashamed of my desire for her.

"Here," Bob said, handing me a small box wrapped in

plastic. "Have these handy and it will happen."

I took the condoms, shook the box, and tossed them in my sock drawer.

After the paint dried, we hung thick cloth curtains over the bedroom windows. The room immediately became filled with shadows and then darkness. It was just the way I wanted it. The paint and curtains would prevent light from entering my childhood bedroom. Now, I could write and plot in secret.

"Remember," Bob said, picking up the paint can and getting ready to leave. "Make a move. Otherwise, you will lose her."

I started to plan how to get some. I wasn't ready, but I had to be, right? Otherwise, I thought, I will lose her, and she meant everything to me.

Then, it happened, suddenly. We did it and then did it again. The pleasure was great for me, but I wasn't sure about her. She bled a little and then she went to clean up in the bathroom. When she came back, we stared at each other again. Neither one of us seemed to know what to say. She got up and left. I was all alone.

In private, I cried. I felt awful. I pulled the curtains together as tight as they would go. The darkness deepened. If sex was so great, why did I feel so terrible afterwards?

I wanted to be with her, but the pleasure of sex did not seem to be the solution. Our friends knew we had sex and that made us feel worse, not better. I thought it was supposed to be some sort of victory, but I was ashamed.

Our conversations became desperate. We wanted to be together again and again, but instead there was only sadness, longing, wanting, and guilt. We were not adults. We did not live together. Instead, we did as our parents told us to do. We had no control.

The problem of sex was that afterwards there was the lack of sex. The union had a promise of further union that could not be met. Only sadness followed. Jeannie and I found ourselves crying on the phone. We would plan to be together but then the plans would fail. Me wanting, her not. Her wanting, me not.

The 'victory' led to complete failure! I had sex with her because I feared losing her. Instead it led to the thing I dreaded the most: losing her. It was only many years later I would discover that most young teenagers are not having sex. I gave in to fake peer pressure. I felt tricked by forked-tongued lies but did not know the source of the lies … at least, not yet.

Chapter 7
Farewells
1986

"You spent so much time alone with Jeannie, nature took its course," Mom explained, holding my shoulders.

My head was down. I nodded.

"Here, vegetable beef, your favorite," Mom slid the bowl of warm soup in front of me.

I shook my head.

"Wheeh!" blew the kettle whistle.

Mom got up, turned off the burner. Steam puffed, and then subsided. She poured me a cup of tea, slid that in front of me. Mom went to the kitchen counter. I reached for the phone.

"No," said Mom. "Let her go. She's no good for you."

I shook my head. "Everything is 'No' with the Catholics! I want to be with her."

"There are some wonderful 'yeses,'" Mom said, "like marriage."

I pictured Mom and Dad yelling at each other in one of their many arguments. I did not want that. But maybe their problem was that Mom was Catholic and Dad was agnostic. Jeannie and I were neither of those. Maybe we could make it better?

"When can I marry her?" I asked.

"Patience is a virtue," Mom said.

Patience? When every second felt like an hour? Every day was a year? How long? How long would I have to wait? I bought a cheapo engagement ring I planned to give to Jeannie. A million times I planned how I would ask for her hand in marriage. Instead…

"Go on now, get it over with," Mom said.

"I can't," I whispered.

"We've already been over this again and again. Now, you will be going to college next year and you cannot have this girl holding you back."

I opened my mouth to speak, but nothing came out. I slowly opened the door and walked to Jeannie's front door. The door was open. In the kitchen, Jeannie sat at the table with her mom and dad.

"Hi, Paul," her dad said.

Jeannie's eyes were huge, staring at me. Her mom looked down. In my head, I imagined giving her the engagement ring. Instead, the plastic engagement ring was already getting picked up by the garbage man.

I set down the gifts Jeannie had given me as instructed, and I quietly left.

I walked back to my mom's car with my head down. I felt so embarrassed and ashamed.

"There," Mom said. "Now, you can put all that behind you."

The sense of failure was hard to put behind me. I wanted social acceptance, material wealth, and sexual satisfaction, all of which had driven me to reject Catholicism and place myself as a self-governing "god."

Yet, the only solution I could see to my Jeannie dilemma was to reject her or to marry her. Marriage? That was a Catholic sacrament. Yet, I saw that as one path to happiness. How could that be?

****

"I'm not going!" Mom whispered.

"You've got to calm down," Dad whispered back, but I overheard them.

"No," Mom said.

Dad stormed out of the house, got on his motorcycle and vroomed away. He had been trying to cover up Mom's breakdowns for years. Only now had the cracks in the system shown through to me.

"Paul," Melissa said, "I'll walk my friends to the bridge. Meanwhile, do something with Mom!"

She left. I wanted to shout after her, "Do what?" How had this become my problem?

"Mom," I said, rubbing my hands together and looking past her.

She was moving plates from one pile to another. "Yes."

"It's time to visit Grandma," I said. "Get your purse and belongings."

"Oh?" she turned to me, her chapped lips showing through her lipstick. "Will I be staying a while?"

"Yes, Mom," I said. "I think so."

She grabbed a few things and we got into the car. I drove to the hospital.

"Where is Grandma?" she said.

"In there," I lied, pointing to the ER entrance.

We went in. After a quick evaluation, two men in white gowns grabbed Mom and placed Mom on a gurney.

"No!" she cried out, struggling.

"Mom!" I reached for her, but there was nothing I could do. As they pulled her out of view, I allowed my hands to fall at my sides.

I drove home in silence. Once home, I threw some chicken into the oven to fix dinner for my younger siblings. I was shaking as I tried to measure out flour. I couldn't remember what I was trying to make to go with the chicken. I put away the flour. I could smell smoke coming from the oven. I pulled the chicken out of the oven. The tops of the pieces were charred black.

I put the overcooked chicken, some creamed potato flakes, canned beans, and peas on the table. I was not sure what to do next. I ran to the bathroom, locked the door and lay on the floor. I fell asleep.

"Let's go, Paul," Dad said.

I woke up on the bathroom floor. The door was open, and Dad stood there over me.

I cringed. "Okay."

We drove to the hospital.

"She can go to Utica or Oswego for further treatment," Dad explained. "I'm going to recommend Utica because it is easier to visit her."

"But Oswego has better care," I replied. "I want her to decide where she goes."

Dad threw his hands into the air, "If that is what you think but…"

"We'll let Mom decide." I said firmly. I believed Mom would want to go to Oswego and Dad was wrong advising her to stay in Utica.

Dad dropped me off at the hospital and waited in the car. I went in and saw Mom. She looked withered.

"Mom," I said.

"Paul!" Her eyes lit up.

"They are telling me you can go to Oswego or stay here in Utica for treatment. Which one do you want?"

"Utica," she said. "Last time I was in Oswego, they gave me too many drugs." What? When had she been there before?

"Okay," I said. I was sure she would say Oswego. Maybe Dad knew more than I gave him credit for? Maybe the house was a mess and the meals burned because of mom's illness preventing her from cleaning and cooking properly? I shook my head. All of that was explainable with a chemical imbalance. Mom loved me when she was able and that was what mattered to me. I did not know then that her faith was behind her love, but I respected her for showing me motherly love.

I glanced at my father. My dad was a different story, complicated.

Dad and I did not speak on the ride home. We got out of the car.

He paused, noticed I was staring at him.

"Let's go for a walk," said Dad.

"Okay," I said.

We started walking up the street.

"Nice weather," he said.

"Yeah," I said, stunned. This was one of only a few times he spoke to me.

"How's Jeannie?" he asked.

"We broke up weeks ago."

"Oh," he said.

"You excited about college?" he asked.

"Yeah," I said.

"Okay," he said, glancing toward the playground. "Go ahead and play. We'll talk again sometime."

"Okay," I said, even though I knew I was too old to play. I ran away from him and climbed up the slide. I would miss that rusty old slide. I probably knew it better than I had known my dad.

I turned back, but Dad had already walked back down the street and out of sight.

****

The summer was hot. Eventually, Mom came back home. She was herself again.

"Dad told me how you spoke while walking up the street to the playground," she said.

"Yeah, so?" I asked.

"He said he explained why he had to beat you up as a kid and you had agreed with him."

"What?" I asked. "We did not talk about that," I said shaking my head no.

We laughed.

Dad lied so often that I wondered if he believed his own lies.

A new-looking car pulled up in our stone driveway. It was Uncle Joe and Aunt Erin.

Mom hugged me, "Good luck in college."

I grabbed my duffle bag and headed off with my aunt and uncle to my new life.

How had Dad invented a conversation that had not happened? I walked myself through our brief talk again and again and could not see how Dad thought we talked about anything other than small talk. He seemed to have a hard time telling the truth. Mom seemed to have a hard time staying in reality.

What would their issues mean for my future? Were their issues caused by circumstances, did I carry their defects in my genes, or both? Thankfully, my siblings were doing well, for the most part, so far…

Chapter 8
Worshipping Science
1987, Long Island, NY

"So, then I worked my ab muscles…" Jay droned on, leaning on his dorm room's bunkbed.

I lay in bed, very still, hoping this would lead my roommate to stop talking.

"So, what are you studying?" Jay asked.

"Biology," I replied, glad the conversation had shifted from his endless workout stories.

"Cool, why?" Jay asked.

"Because . . ." I started, staring at the ceiling. Did I really know why I chose biology? "I think if I study the beauty of earth's creatures: flora, fauna, and human, that I can get to the heart of what determines people's thoughts and actions."

"How's that?" Jay lay on his bed and turned to me.

"Well, if I learn about the physical body, then I will know how the mind works."

"Yeah, health of the body matters—" Jay started.

I cut him off quickly before he told me more about his workout regimen. "And that the right ideas can lead to a better mankind and a more orderly society."

"Huh?" Jay pondered. "Sounds like sociology."

"Sociobiology," I corrected him. "Past civilizations failed to understand human nature and that encouraged corruption stemming from a desire for power and control."

"Isn't that the role of religion?" Jay asked.

"No!" I yelled. "Religions are attempts to control

people as the 'opiate of the masses.'" I made air quotes with my hands.

"Maybe false religions but Catholics…" Jay started.

"Roman Catholicism is no more than an extension of the fallen Roman Empire to continue to influence society by clericalism." Did I really believe that, or were these the words of my father from his living room pulpit?

Jay frowned. "So, you think all religions are a bad idea?"

"Religions cause wars!" Was these not also my father's or older brother Michael's words? I went on anyway, determined to take their words a step further. "Religion is one of the bad ideas that lead to the horrors of injustice and ultimately to torture and death."

Jay sighed, "So, what do you think is the answer?"

"Science," I said, smiling. "The logic and reproducibility of the western scientific method is the only true way to influence society to improve mankind."

Jay paused to cover himself up with his blanket. "It sounds like you have a love affair with science."

"No," I snapped back, "I just believe science can explain all things."

"Like what?"

"Science alone can explain my mother's illness. Also, I feel science is a high-demand field that I can build a career in and become part of the middle class."

"So, you think you can cure your mom and make money?" he asked.

"Maybe Mom will not be cured in her lifetime, but future generations will not have to suffer the way she does because of science. I will leave poverty behind and enter the middle class with a science education, and even if the jobs are not what I expect them to be, I will be better off due to science."

"I don't know, Paul" Jay said. "It seems like you might be setting yourself up for a huge disappointment."

"Wherever I end up," I told him, "it will be better than where I came from."

****

"I'm taking abnormal psychology," Patrick said. He stood at the cereal dispenser and turned the plastic knob to let Fruit Loops fall into his white foam cereal bowl.

"Cool," I said, thinking of my parents. I went for the Apple Jacks.

"How about you?" Patrick asked as he lifted his tray.

"Outside my major?" I asked, following him to a table in the college's cafeteria.

He nodded.

"German culture. Also, African culture."

"Why those?" he asked.

"I want to see how very different cultures work," I said, taking a drink of orange juice.

"To what end?" he asked.

"I figure all humans have the same biology. Should there not emerge then from different cultures overlapping themes of natural law?"

"Like what?" he asked, sipping his coffee.

"Like no murder, no rape, no theft, etc...."

"Isn't that the role of organized religion?"

"Does it have to be?" I asked, raising my voice.

"I don't know," Patrick shrugged. "I like learning

about weird human behavior."

"Yeah," I said, thankful to change the topic. "Is that how abnormal psychology is defined?"

"Simplistically, yeah."

"Seems a far cry from electrical engineering," I said.

"Any more than foreign culture is from biology?" Patrick asked.

We laughed.

While the culture classes did give me some sense of human behavior in groups, I still wondered where moral ideas came from.

****

"Why are you taking Comparative Religions?" Stephen said, looking at my textbook.

"I just want to see what is in common among religions," I replied.

"What religions?"

"The seven so-called great world religions: Taoism, Confucianism, Buddhism, Hinduism, Islam, Judaism, and Christianity."

"Why in that order?" he asked.

"I don't know—that is the order in which they are presented in the textbook."

"Seems like they put Christianity last, as if it is the conclusion," Stephen pointed out.

"Yeah," I said, "and not the problem."

We laughed.

"Seems like those ideas just interfere with what I want to do," said Stephen.

"What do you want to do?"

"Party, drink, have sex, get what I want, stuff."

I laughed. "You always get right to it!"

"Yup," he said, smiling.

"What about the sadness afterwards?" I asked, my eyebrows furrowed.

"After what?" he asked.

"After doing those kinds of things, I feel sad, lonely and empty again."

"That's just left-over guilt from your Catholic upbringing," he offered.

"No. It just seems like I feel like more of a failure."

"That don't mean much," he said. "If you do it again, the pain will go away. Enjoy the good times. Don't overthink it!"

"Maybe," I said, "but I'm taking this class to see if there are any common themes among these seven great religions."

Stephen took a swig from a beer bottle. "It's your life. Go for it."

"Well," Stephen said a few weeks later, while placing another empty bottle on top of our beer bottle pyramid in our dorm room corner, "what have you learned?"

I was reading from the last third of my world great religions book.

"I've learned there are some common themes and some new ideas from each of the first six religions I've read about so far."

"Like what?" Stephen said, reaching into the mini-fridge for another beer.

"Taoism teaches a way of life that is very practical," I started.

"Practical?"

"Yeah, common sense stuff to balance your life and not be too materialistic."

"Hmph," said Stephen, "that don't mean much. I can do that for myself." He twisted the top off and took a swig of beer.

"Yeah, I can see that," I said, trying to be sarcastic, yet trying also to point out his alcoholic behavior.

"What else?" he asked.

"Confucianism teaches how people should interact," I offered.

"Interact? Like have sex?" Stephen rubbed his hands together.

I laughed. "Well, it is concerned with who you can and cannot have sex with, yes."

"Waste of time," he said.

"Buddhism goes a step further by suggesting we care about others."

"Yeah, as long as they care about us."

"Well, kind of, that is utilitarianism or the golden rule at its best."

"So," he scoffed.

"Hinduism teaches that we must accept our circumstances in life."

"Do we have any choice?" he asked.

"I suppose we can fight against fate, or not give into, or believe, in fate."

"I suppose," he said, lying on his bed.

"Those four religions are all polytheistic, where there are multiple gods. They are sort of like the dead beliefs of Egyptian, Greek, Norse, and Roman gods. These all would be considered paganisms to those that worship one God."

"Hmph."

"Islam, while monotheistic, is an even harsher form of fatalism, where one must give in to the role given to us by Allah."

"That stinks," Stephen said.

"It is what it is," I laughed.

"Yeah, all religions are crazy," he said.

"Well, I'm not so sure I'd go that far," I replied.

"What else?"

"Judaism has one God, Yahweh, who came up with rules and doles out justice."

"Sounds like a way to instill fear," he said.

"It might prevent some heinous crimes like murder," I suggested.

"Naw," he said, "the threat of getting caught, imprisoned, tortured and killed does that."

"Yet, murder still happens," I said.

"Yup," Stephen said, "by those who think they will get away with it."

"I can see how and why man made up these religions."

"What do you mean?" Stephen asked.

"Each religion has heroes, a god or gods, and stories, like superhero comic books. There is a human author who is benefiting from each of these ideas."

"How so?"

"I can see how, and why, these religions were made up by people. For example, the Greek gods showed greed; the Roman gods showed loss; the Viking gods showed glory. These ideas are what I would share if I wanted to control a population from rebellion."

"Yup," Stephen said.

"And I see a common flaw. These religions in no way bind me to do, or not do, anything anymore than human laws and punishments would."

"So, what?"

****

"You should embrace Christianity," Donna held my arm as we walked along the campus trail discussing the classes we were taking.

"Well, I do find the Christian faith puzzling because it does not make sense to me."

"How so?" she asked.

"I can see how other religions could be made up by people, but not Christianity. It seems strange and alien."

"Alien?" she scrunched up her face.

"Yes, Christianity does not seem made up by mankind."

"I agree. I'm Christian." She intertwined her fingers in mine. "Are you sure you're not saying this just to flirt?"

"No," I said. "I do see Christianity as alien. I mean, wow, so God became man so that he could be tortured, and crucified?"

"Yes, he did, but for a reason."

"It seems like other religions focus on what people want, such as joy, and their gods seem to get whatever they want and those who follow their path get whatever they want in this life."

"They offer a bunch of empty promises," she said.

"Christianity makes no such promise. In fact, it seems to say just the opposite: if I became a Christian, I would be persecuted and must follow Christ to be tortured to death. Then supposedly my reward would be in the afterlife."

"No, silly, you just have to accept Jesus into your heart as your Savior. I was saved on October 7, 1981. Are you saved?" Donna said.

"Saved? I'm not sure, I was raised Catholic."

"Oh no!" she said.

"What?" I asked.

"Catholics are not Christians."

"I think they are," I said, wondering why I cared if they were, or not.

"No, they are not. Catholics worship statues…"

"Anyway, I am an atheist now," I said quickly. I was pretty sure Catholics did not worship statues, but why did I care one way or the other?

Donna paused, then smiled. "An atheist studying Christianity?" she said.

"It's just the one class," I said. "I do not believe that God exists."

"Why take the class then?"

"To understand human group behavior."

"But you admit Christianity is somehow different from the rest?"

"I see Christ as a philosopher, but I do not believe Christ performed miracles or rose from the dead."

"He came to free us. Don't you want that?" she asked.

"I am free," I said. "Free from religion."

"Then you are free of me!" Donna stormed off.

I did not follow her then.

Chapter 9
College Crushed
1989

"You can go to the party," Craig said, "if you bring that." He pointed to my beer watermill wall hanging.

I nodded, picked it up, and carried the dumb thing down the hallway.

Craig's doorway was jammed with people. Inside, girls were hanging onto each other, hanging on to guys, holding up the walls, and stomping on the floor. Neon lights highlighted wall posters. Guys pecked at beer nuts. Craig manned the keg.

"Ah!" Craig said. "You brought the beer mill."

"Beer mill guy!" the room cheered.

I set it down and waved.

That girl was there, staring at me, the one who looked like an adult version of Jeannie. I gasped. She and I stared at each other. I couldn't escape her gaze.

"Corrie!" Craig shouted. "Yeah," he looked around, "she will gladly inaugurate you for us, won't you, Corrie?"

She smiled. The crowd laughed. Corrie gawked at me like she was about to eat me for dinner. I fled.

Music and lights came from each room. I went room to room trying out the drinks. In one hall, between rooms, I spotted Tamra, another Jeannie look-alike. Her boyfriend Greg was nowhere in sight.

"Hi, Tamra," I said.

She waved half-heartedly.

"Where's Greg?" I asked.

"We broke up," she said, covering her face.

I sat next to her. "It's okay."

Under her hands, I could see she was grinning. She leaned towards me and kissed me!

What? She was Greg's girlfriend. Did they break up? I did not believe her. I tried to get up.

She grabbed my hand and pulled me down. We kissed again. I stood up again. This time I grabbed her hand and pulled her up. We put our arms around each other and went to a few more rooms, trying green liquor, yellow wine, etc.... until I lost sight of her.

Somehow, I stumbled back to my room. I fell on my bed and dreamed. My friends and I were jumping into a snow pile. It was my turn. The snow came up to my forehead. I could not breathe. Then I opened my eyes. I was covered with shaving cream and could barely move. Vaguely, I remember the sound of a sprayer.

Andy and Joe picked me up and put me in the shower. The water freed me. They dried me off and put me back in my bed.

Next morning, I hung my jeans and shirt to dry in the bathroom, got dressed, and did the walk of shame down the dorm elevator to the cafeteria.

I saw Andy and Joe and the gang sitting at the usual table. There was a spot for me, but I walked past them and went to sit with my roommate Jay and his hockey buddies. They snickered when I sat down. I ate silently, eyeing Andy and Joe's table.

After eating, I went to the mail room. There I saw Greg and Tamra kissing. When they saw me, Greg waved and Tamra smiled. With a dead look in her eyes, Tamra looked through me as though we had not kissed last night. They held hands and walked away. Back together, I should have known.

Andy was standing beside me. "It wasn't us," he said.

"I saw you!" I said.

"Saw me what?" he asked.

My eyes widened as I recalled seeing him shower me.

"It was those hockey guys you sat with just now who foamed you up, not us," Andy said.

I knew instantly he was right. Andy and Joe found me smothered in shaking cream foam and put me in the shower to clean me up.

"You were hazed," he said. "You gotta know who to trust." Andy sighed and then walked away.

I felt like a dodo bird. *How could I know who to trust?*

****

"Go with the Moo!" said Patrick.

"Go with it!" Ross, Stephen and I replied.

Ross had attached his bong to the hamster cage. Smoke still billowed out of the top of the wire net cover.

The hamster danced tentatively around on the saw dust, its eyes and nose bulging out of its face.

Four new faces were in Ross's room: a slightly pudgy guy with a five o'clock shadow; a Greek guy with slicked-back hair; and two women, both cute brunettes.

"This is Samuel, Damon, Silvia, and Karen," Patrick said.

We all shook hands. Josh sat next to Silvia. I stood by Karen. Patrick handed Samuel and Damon beers.

"Bamboo forest?" Patrick said.

Ross, Stephen and I jumped up and gave Patrick and each other high fives. We were four guys who trusted each other with drugs, alcohol, women, and fun. We ran out to the hallway. The others followed, shrugging their shoulders and laughing.

We ran down the stairwell, mooing like cows all the way down to the ground, "Moo! Moooooo! Moo!"

Outside, we dashed into the woods. There were maple trees, evergreens, and even bamboo.

"How did bamboo get here?" Samuel asked.

"Genetically engineered to withstand the temperate zone," I replied quickly running along, holding Karen's hand.

"Whoooooooo!" said Karen.

"The fire pit is up ahead somewhere," said Patrick.

"Ah!" Damon fell over a fallen tree trunk, then got up and kept running.

"How are we able to see in the woods?" Samuel asked.

"Foxfire," I said, tickling Karen as we ran.

"What's that?" Samuel kept pace besides me.

"Fluorescent fungi."

Samuel looked around. A light green glow came from patches on the ground and at the base of the trees. "All night?" he asked.

"No, it wears off," I said.

"Here's the fire pit," Stephen said.

We gathered dead wood, which was easy to spot because it glowed from fungi eating at its insides and built a huge bonfire. It burned so brightly that we could see the slightest imperfections in each other's faces from the warm glow.

Karen kissed me. We embraced, smiled, and then put our arms around each other's shoulders, watching the fire.

"Fire jumping!" Josh screamed, leaping over the bonfire, while flames licked at his sneakers, bare arms, and shirt coat tails.

"Opah!" Damon shouted, not realizing he had just added to our mumbo jumbo language.

Patrick jumped next. His long legs easily leapt over the flames.

"Opah!" We all shouted.

"Is he okay?" Karen asked me.

"No," I said. "He's nuts, but a great friend, totally trustworthy."

She laughed. "You trust a crazy person?"

I nodded. "This is my gang. Take us as is or leave us all."

"I take you," she said, touching my chest.

Stephen jumped next.

"Opah!" we yelled.

"Go, Moo-man," Patrick said, patting me on the shoulder.

I backed away from the fire, ran, jumped, and closed my eyes.

"Opah!"

I felt the heat.

Karen pulled me away by my shirt from the fire pit. "How can you do that?"

"Hey," I said, removing her hand from my shirt. "We Moo-men love each other. What more can there be?"

Karen smiled, "I'll show you." She grabbed my hand and pulled me into the woods.

I turned back only to see Josh give me the Moo-man thumbs up. He was holding onto Silvia and looking for a chance to escape the group as well.

I tripped over Karen as we ran into the woods. I fell

hard but laughed. We undressed each other, wrestling and laughing. We explored each other on the dirty ground, like earthworms mating, throughout most of the night.

About four a.m., the fluorescence started to fade, and we could barely see. It was getting cold, even though we were holding on to each other, so we quickly got dressed.

"I can't hear them anymore," she said.

"They're probably sleeping now," I said.

"Should we head back?" Karen asked.

"Nah," I said, "It'll be sunrise soon enough."

"How do you know so much about the forest?" Karen asked.

"I'm studying biochemistry. Right now, I'm taking ethnobotany."

"If you're so smart," she asked, pinching my arm, "why do you hang out with those goons?"

"Those goons," I said, pinching her side, "are the smartest engineering students I've ever met."

"Oh, yeah?" she said, in a fake baritone guy voice.

"Yeah," I said, "Ross can get an A on a test—even while totally drunk."

"That's just plain stupid."

"We know each other. We trust each other. We're the Moo-men."

She grunted, "Back to the whole male bonding thingy…"

"Man is a social animal," I said. "We need community, a group we can trust."

"What," she said mockingly, "like a motorcycle gang?"

I frowned. My dad rode a motorcycle; I resented motorcycle riders.

"I'm just kidding," Karen whispered in my ear.

"It is logical," I said. "Humans are a pile of chemicals. Our social behavior is dictated by our evolutionary path. The highest state humans can reach is community."

"A pile of chemicals," she mocked, putting her hands into quotes.

"Yes," I said, "I'm an atheist."

"Well then," she said, "so am I. Now let's form our own communion?" she raised her eyebrows and then kissed me.

I felt confused. I wanted her approval. My friends, the self-named Moo-men, were smart and hard working. They were A students with bright futures. I loved them. I wanted her to love them as I loved them and to accept all their behaviors.

My community seemed enough to me now, but she seemed to be suggesting there was more to life. What could there be more than community? I thought of a motorcycle gang. No, we were more than thugs. We were a community with rules and codes of behavior. That was what set us apart from my dad. Except, there were times when even I found myself pulling away from the Moo-men's more reprehensible behaviors.

****

I decided to visit the campus health center to try to sort out the warring voices in my head.

"Tell me about your childhood," the counselor started.

I sat back in my chair and rambled for an hour. I shared some sad stuff.

Sessions came and went until finally he presented me with a "study all the time to professionalism" path that he said would lead to my own personal freedom.

"But what is the purpose of freedom?" I asked.

"Well," he said, "to do as you wish. Like you said, you have a community of friends, you enjoy fun, drinking, and sex with girls."

"What about the sadness I feel afterwards?" I asked

"That is just a remnant of guilt from your Catholic upbringing."

I'd heard that so often before that I ignored it. "Or maybe the need for a community to have rules?" I suggested.

He nodded. "Rules are good to protect people."

"And communal living, like cities, to thrive," I said.

"Yes, to flourish, people specialize and help each other," he replied.

"But," I said, "but my dad believes in those things and does not thrive."

"I have heard everything you have told me about your dad." He leaned forward. "You have to accept that your dad is not interested in you and wants to live his own life."

I swallowed. That hurt, but it was the sting of truth. Yet, it contradicted the advantages of communal living. Was my dad wrong? Was the counselor wrong? What were there rules of living? Were there any rules at all?

If there were no real rules, then maybe the purpose of life was just selfishness. The only two realities were that I existed and that I was going to die. So I needed to grab hold of as much pleasure as I possibly could in this short life and do as much as I could for myself as I had come to conclude, right or wrong, that my father had done for himself.

When I came home from college that summer, that was very much confirmed as my father had left my mother and was dating a nurse. He rode his motorcycle right into the proverbial sunset. I wasn't sure if he went through a midlife crisis or something like that, but soon after that, my parents divorced.

This led me to believe I was completely on my own and that no one helped anyone else. Also, I thought, even if God exists, he would be like my father and not care about anyone but his own self-interests. I concluded that I must maximize my experience and success in life, no matter whom or what I had to step over, or on top of, to do it.

As much as I did not want to be like my father, he was the only role model I had. Maybe he had the right idea after all?

****

So, I partied hard, but studied harder. I would go to a party, see my friends, have one beer, and then disappear to the library until two a.m. to study every weekday and all weekend. By this life of duality, I pulled my grades up towards the top of the class.

I had concluded from my dad's behavior that the purpose of life was to just live with someone and enjoy your time in this life with that person. So, I started living with a woman named Phoebe.

"I'm a witch," she said, smiling at me.

I laughed, "What level?"

"Huh?" she said.

"Oh, D&D," I said.

"What's D&D?"

"*Dungeons and Dragons*," I said.

"Oh, role playing..." she smiled. "No, not like that."

"So, do you mean like a costume on Halloween, you dress up as a witch?"

"No, I am a witch," she said.

"Really?"

"When I lived in Philly, a group of us would dress up as witches and actually decided to become witches. It's fun!"

"Oh," I said, startled, but trying to look confident in front of a stunningly beautiful young woman.

Maybe something remained of my Catholic identity because I was disturbed when she showed me pictures of her in a black outfit with a black hat.

"I'll not be a witch, if you will not be a Catholic," Phoebe said, and I agreed, but it bothered me. Why did it matter that I not be a Catholic? It stuck in my mind somehow that the two were opposites, one worshiping the devil, even though not admitting to it, and the other worshiping God in His church. Also, why did I care that she not be a witch, even if she were a Satanic worshipper? If there was no God, then there was also no devil. Why did it matter what she did?

"The Catholic Church," I told her, "was an attempt of the Roman Empire to continue its power in the world." I'm embarrassed now to even admit that I thought such a vile thing, but I did.

"Why do you attack the Catholic faith, and no other religion?" she asked me.

"They make the most demands on people," I said.

"Okay," she said, "but why not attack all religions? Why single out Catholicism?"

I did wonder why I attacked Catholicism. I had to admit that I believed that there was something special and unique about the Catholic faith.

One thing we agreed on was that we thought there was no supernatural nonsense. There was no supernatural; there was no devil or God; no heaven or hell, and therefore no reason to care either way.

Yet, I did care, and it did matter. I just couldn't figure out why.

****

"What's wrong?" Phoebe asked.

I held my left arm up in the air. "I'm not sure."

"Why are you doing that?"

"My heartbeat faded. I cannot hear it anymore."

"What does that have to do with your arm?" she asked, touching my back.

"The blood stopped flowing."

"We've got to get you to the emergency room!"

I shook my head. "I don't have insurance."

"What should we do then?" she asked.

"Just wait," I said, "it will pass." Would it? I really didn't know, but luckily it did pass in a few minutes.

Phoebe helped me lay down. She propped up my head with a pillow, made tea from her electric pot and poured us both a cup. She spoke to me in a smooth, soothing voice.

This sickness, and others, struck me several times in my senior year. Each time, Phoebe was there to comfort me. While not my mom, her care for me reminded me of how my mom cared for me the numerous days I was at home sick from high school. The many times that Phoebe/Mom held me, rubbed my back, fed me, sang to me, and spent time with me kept me alive inside. When I found this girl, who would take care of me like my mom did. I thought she was the girl for me. But was she?

Chapter 10
Dispossessed Graduate

1991, Evanston, IL

Phoebe and I were hanging out at a sidewalk café, both of us busy studying. I sipped my coffee, skimming the biochemistry tome in front of me as she perused her art history text.

"I'm getting more time in the spectroscopy center."

"What does that mean?" she asked.

"I'll be working until midnight, maybe even two a.m., and getting up at six a.m. to start all over every day for the next month."

"Well, if that is what it takes," Phoebe said.

"It is, if I intend to go for my doctorate."

"Is there any question that you will not do so?" she said.

"No," I said, "I mean, yes, I plan to get my PhD."

"Good," she said.

We finished our drinks and walked back to our apartment complex holding hands. Fireflies were flickering on the grounds. Courtyard lights turned on as the shadows deepened. The bushes and flowers sparkled in the light from a recent watering. Inside, she held me, and we embraced. I held her back to gaze at her face.

"I thought we would go visit my family?" I asked, somewhat pleadingly.

"Why would we do that?" she snapped back. "Last time was a disaster."

We took a step back from each other.

"A disaster? It was unpleasant, but how was it a disaster?"

"Remember, your mom and your sister made us sleep separately."

"Oh, yeah," I whispered. "Was it really that bad?"

"Yes!" she yelled, "Of course, it was bad. Also, I feel like I must take care of your mom, your brother, and your sister when I go there."

"You do?" I asked.

"Of course. They do not do anything the right way," she folded her arms.

Oh, I wondered, *what is the right way?*

"We have each other. What do we need your family for?" She kissed me.

Maybe she was right. Maybe not.

****

I'm outdoors in a wheat field at night... I float up into the air, up through the clouds… The moisture of the rainy mist chills my skin… Above the clouds now, I see the moon's reflection on the top of the clouds…. I whisk through the clouds down above a city of night lights from high-rise buildings…. This is a dream? This is a dream. I can go anywhere I like then. What if I wanted to hover back in the field just above the ground? … Then, as fast as I thought it, it happened. I am just barely hovering above the ground, with my feet inches above the surface.

I sat up and screamed, "Ahhh!"

I felt Phoebe's hand on my shoulder and heard her soft voice. "What is it?"

"Ah! Ah!"

She hugged me. "Calm down! It was just a dream."

I breathed heavily, then slower. "Yes, just a dream, but it felt like it was real."

"What happened?"

"I floated above the ground by just a few inches, simply by willing it," I explained.

She relaxed, let go of me and leaned back. "So?"

"So? Not only could I fly, but I teleported to the exact spot I thought about instantaneously."

She moved a strand of hair from my face. "So, what?"

"It seemed wrong," I said.

Phoebe shrugged her shoulders. "You've been getting better at controlling your dreams for some time now…"

"I know," I said, shakily, "but the jumping and flying seemed out of my control, then I could decide when and where I would land, but this time…"

"… you could do what you wanted?" she smiled.

"Yes," I got up from the bed, "and I'll never do that again." It was too much control, and it felt like the control came from something else, something dark.

She frowned, lay down, and closed her eyes.

I stumbled to the kitchen, got out a glass, poured some orange juice and sat staring out the window at the streetlamp. After some time, I relaxed and collapsed onto the couch.

It seemed to me there were no limits to my imagination, but I wanted limits. I wanted to reside within my creations, but with limits. But why?

****

The standing lamp was turned down to a warm glow. A flicker swayed from the top of a candle on the night stand. She touched me gently. "So, we go on a trip next weekend?"

I flinched. "I don't know yet. It depends on my lab experiment."

She let go of me. I could read the disappointment all over her face.

I placed my hand on her shoulder. "No, wait! I can shift some of the time slots in the lab to free me up next weekend."

She touched me again, smiling. "Mmmmm," she held me tighter, "what else, let me think…I want Mom and Dad to visit next month, okay?"

"Next month! I have a doctoral committee review next month."

She pulled away again and stood next to the night stand which highlighted her curved silhouette.

"But…of course! I'll be busy, so you can spend time with your parents."

Phoebe moved toward me smoothly. "That's it! And you will do lab work, not go out with your friends."

"Yes," I said.

She pulled me to her.

****

Friends and family started to withdraw from us. I would ask them why, and all they would say is "We do not like her."

"Oh," I would reply, "that's too bad."

"I'll pray for you," my mom would say. Why would she pray for us? It didn't matter if she did. It was just talking to the air. There was no one to listen or care, right?

We started to become isolated from people. While this was good for my degree, because I could spend long hours in the lab, it was bad for us, especially me. All the people that mattered to me were fading away. Only Phoebe remained. Even then, I knew her goal was to get me alone.

Sometimes I would think, "...and then what?" One time the thought occurred to me, "...to kill me."

I still had affection for her, and I did not take this train of thought seriously, but I was concerned. I wondered if she had the power to harm someone: me or herself, or someone else. I wondered if I could get ever get away from this situation. Did I want to?

Chapter 11
Intermission
1992

The day my brother Matt turned eighteen, I sent him a very unusual birthday card.

"Congratulations, Matt!

Your brain has been growing...

(A series of pictures displayed an evolving brain.)

Now you have a complete brain.

Use it well!"

Matt visited me in Chicago in the summertime. I gave him a tour of the Windy City. We spent a great deal of time at the Chicago museums.

I tried to give my brother advice. "Now that you'll be entering the real world, I think it is time you said goodbye to the Imaginary Universe. Look around you, here is the history of the real world. The dinosaurs, the mammals and plants, the American Indians, art history, modern science and much, much more. Do with it what you will, young man."

"I do wonder, though," Matt said, "how did all this life appear on earth?"

"Science," I said, "that is how. Evolution, billions of years, that's how."

"Oh, yeah," Matt said, throwing his hands up in the air, "that really explains it."

We laughed. Although, I frowned because I already knew at this point in my life that the Cambrian explosion was an evolutionarily narrow band of time in which single cell organisms suddenly became all the body forms we see in Earth's creatures today… and no scientific theory was able to explain this.

Matt liked the displays, but it got to be a bit too educational for a summer vacation. The day Matt was to return to New York, I took him to a local basketball court.

"For old times' sake, how about one more basketball tournament?"

"Okay."

I had to play Matt without holding back. For the first time, the height advantage went to Matt. He won the championship, fair and square, exhausting his older, shorter brother.

That night, Matt packed, and I called a taxi.

"Remember to tell the taxi driver which airline you're taking."

"Got it," Matt said, weighing the luggage in his hands. "Well, goodbye. It was fun."

"Goodbye and best of luck in college. We'll stay in touch by email."

Matt laughed but looked a little sad. In our Imaginary Universe, Matt had been a rock star, a soldier, an adventurer, a sports champion, a hero, a king and even an emperor. Now, he was just a scared young man going away to college.

I hoped that everything in the Imaginary Universe had taught Matt a lesson about life. He knew the difference between good and evil because he had been on both sides of the rope. He knew how power could corrupt. I'm pretty sure all he wanted was a sane life.

Matt got in the taxi. I watched him head for the airport as the sun set on the Imaginary Universe.

Chapter 12
Social Implications of Science
1993

"Are you ever going to finish this paper?" Phoebe asked.

"It takes time to see the social implications of future technology," I said.

"Several lifetimes, more like it."

"Aren't you interested in the imaginable technologies and how they affect people?"

She shrugged, dipping her pen into fresh ink and continuing to work on her drawing.

I wanted to make her understand. "See, the wildest future technological ideas might excite people to make and use them, but how would they really work? Would they help people more than they hurt people?"

"Who knows?" she said.

"But that is just it," I replied. "I want to know ahead of time whether mankind is served or harmed."

"Maybe it cannot be known."

"You know I hate the idea that science cannot solve anything."

"Yes," she replied.

"Maybe Dr. Hampton was right."

"How so?"

"He told me that science is moving so fast that we are in an era of living out past generations of science in a few years."

"How can people keep up with that?" She feigned interest.

"We can't. Technology is changing so fast that our social structure cannot keep up."

"Okay, sounds exciting."

"Not necessarily so," I said. "We can reconstruct society in our own image: the creations of mankind can determine how future man looks, acts, thinks, and believes."

"So," she put her pen away.

"So, science and technology become god!" I stated, but I shivered at my own thoughts.

****

"We need to buy you a bookcase," Phoebe said.

She was right. My reading materials were strewn about the table, my desk, and in piles on the floor. I read what I consider to be the top sources of technology and science, especially as it related to human society. In addition to magazines, I read reviews. Critique columns were strewn into the piles.

Then in addition to becoming an avid reader, I became a writer. For me, it was a transformative stage. No longer a chrysalis, I became a butterfly. I wrote whenever I was not working in the lab. First, I wrote about sports medicine for the *Daily Northwestern* with the help and guidance of students in the Medill School of Journalism. After that, I published short stories, poetry, and a novelette. At writers' conferences, I learned that I should keep my day job because very few could support themselves writing.

Still, I persevered. I started a writers' forum called *Writopia* that basically acted as a writers' workshop in pulp magazine form. I eventually became editor of a semiprofessional magazine aptly named *Age of Wonder.*

I was attracted to the idea of finding stories that portrayed a sense of wonder, yet I found myself rejecting all the submitted stories. Many were too simple or were too easily deconstructed. Sometimes I rejected 200 stories in one month. Due to my pickiness, sometimes we did not have anything to publish.

"You have to pick something to be published," Fred said.

"I know," I said.

My Catholic classmate was silent.

"What?" I asked.

"I hope you will not take offense," he said cautiously.

"No, go ahead. I need advice to get this issue published."

Fred said, "You are seeking God."

I froze. "What?!"

He repeated, "You are seeking God."

"Seeking God?" I yelled. "You are only saying that because you are Catholic."

"Calm down," he said.

I lowered my voice. "Just because I am searching for stories with a sense of wonder does not mean that I am seeking God."

"None of those stories will ever fill your need for God."

"What?" I said and left in a huff.

I ended up publishing some known-name authors but with no enthusiasm. Still, I couldn't shake Fred's accusation. I had taken a class in religion and found it interesting. Did that mean I was searching for God? I tried to force myself to reject this idea immediately, but the question continued to bother and annoy me because no matter how much I tried not to, I continued to do just that: seek God.

Chapter 13
Human Limits
1994

"Have faith," Dr. John Choan, my doctoral advisor at Northwestern, said. I met with him once per week to review my experiments. The last several weeks, all my experiments had failed. Several of my classmates who were used to getting "A's" in the classroom had already quit the program due to failures in the laboratory. *Was I next, or would this faith idea help me?*

What was I supposed to have faith in? In the lab, in the experiment, in the scientific method, in him because he had more knowledge and experience than me? Faith in God? I wanted to flee.

But I did not flee because I wanted to be near my advisor. When I would go into his office, he seemed to have a soft glow about him. It wouldn't be until seven years later that I would discover he was a Christian with a wife and three kids. In any case, I was drawn to him and felt grateful to have a good advisor.

I walked back to the lab and sat, staring at a lab bench with my arms folded. It was hard to hear the word "faith."

Finally, I decided that at least wanted to have his 'determination,' if nothing else; but refused to call it 'faith.' So, I kept trying and eventually found a pattern in the data that led to my obtaining a doctorate degree. I, in big part, have my advisor to thank for instilling in me the idea of faith—despite my stubborn resistance.

Did I keep trying because I believed that I could find an answer in nature? That nature somehow has an intrinsic order to it? The problem for me as an atheist at that time was that I did not believe the universe had a maker, or an order, or a natural law, and so it was hard to have faith in anything when I did not have faith in a god.

I had to lean on my advisor for faith in a similar way that my father had to lean on my grandfather for faith. Such an external way of having faith cannot sustain a person, but it was all I had at the time. I was constantly trying to understand the universe by asking who, what, where, when, why? I did believe as a scientist that some ideas are better than others, just as some theories are better than others. I imagined that humans were the results of random postmodern evolution, but also that somehow, we were responsible because of our awareness and therefore somehow culpable. So, I felt that even though humanity was a random creation, mankind had an ordered role of inserting meaning into the universe. I still did not see a god in the picture, but rather, I thought that mankind was the master of his own universe.

My search continued. I would not admit that I was seeking God, but I *was* seeking God. And so, although my faith derived from Dr. Choan's faith was temporary, a storm was brewing.

****

For lunch, I walked through the long straight corridors of the tech building and took a side door to the south loading dock service road. From there, I trudged up a small hill and followed a trail into the woods to the Shakespeare Garden.

Just south of the Shakespeare Garden was the Garret Methodist Seminary. I sat, overhearing some of the seminarians' lunch conversation.

"Einstein's theory of relativity," a taller seminarian explained to another shorter with a beard.

I shook my head but hesitated to speak. His words sounded correct, like he knew physics. But ... how could that be? How could he know physics and become a seminarian who believes in a God?

When they started discussing biochemistry, my field, I decided to join in their conversation.

"Do seminarians routinely discuss science?" I asked them.

They laughed, "Actually," the taller said, "it is our hobby at lunch to pontificate on a number of fields of study."

"Really?" my eyes bulged.

He nodded.

"Okay, tell me then, what is the Endosymbiotic Theory?" I asked.

They stopped laughing. I let the silence wash over them, thinking I had won.

"Evidence suggests," the shorter started coolly," mitochondria and chloroplasts may have once been independent living bacterial cells."

My jaw dropped, "Go on."

"Larger cells, like ah...like amoeba, may have swallowed those smaller cells and then gained energy that helped the big cells survive and get bigger. So 'Endo-' inside of, and '-symbiotic' of mutual benefit."

"Okay," I put my hand to my chin. "Religious study

Latin so you may have taken an educated guess."

They laughed. "That would be a very specific educated guess, don't you think?" asked the taller one.

My face became red, this reminded me of how Protestants made fun of me as a child. I had to prove them wrong, I thought, but never did.

"How does altruism theory show the selfish animal nature of man?"

"It does not," The tall one frowned.

"But the man benefits by helping another who may help him in the future."

"Suppose the other is a child, but not his biological child and he dies in the process of saving this child?" he asked me.

"So-?" I stammered.

"So, there is no evolutionary advantage to him since he has no children and died with no biological children."

"It could help the species." I offered.

"Yes, that is altruism, helping others with nothing gained in return."

"It is still a selfish act," I said meekly.

"How?" he asked.

"He is preserving his species because the child will grow up to be an adult and would have outlived his lifespan anyway."

"But you do not know the child would have outlived the adult. Anyone can die at any time."

"The man is trying to look good or important or something like that..." I said.

"To whom? Suppose there were no human witnesses."

I wanted to say that the man was still selfish, but I

was unable to get the words out.

As time passed, I met them again and again. I was surprised to learn that the seminarians there knew more than I did about math, science, engineering, and history.

How was this possible? I thought.

This did not fit my atheistic belief that religious people were ignorant, weak, and doomed to fail. These people did not join a seminary because they failed. In fact, most of them had been very successful. They explained to me that they considered their chosen career a continued path to success.

I wondered how they could stoop to God worship. How could they believe in God with a capital 'G' yet be rational, logical and reasonable people?

****

I had heard that humanism had a proposed explanation for altruism theory, so I went to work.

I walked to the Charles Deering Memorial Library and started researching humanism. There are so many texts and versions of humanism that I was somewhat confused at first.

Then, I found one aspect of it quite interesting: that man, since he has consciousness, has a duty to create and maintain order and morality in the universe. Could this human desire help to explain altruism theory?

I became okay with the idea of a 'higher power' if the interpretation was the collective intelligence of many people over time. I allowed this concept to be my demi-god. Of course, the problem right away with this approach was that it contradicted much of the other information I was receiving, such as seminarians who know science better than I do.

So what information was correct?

Besides the seminarians I met on campus, I also found off campus many Christians who were logical and rational and had faith. I believed that if they had irrational beliefs, they should have failed, but they were succeeding. I was forced to question the validity of my philosophy, but I still had no better answers yet.

Still, I was not ready to accept a god with an upper-case 'G.' Instead, maybe there was a way I could have some of the social and communal benefits of morality, without the 'magical god' part?

Chapter 14
Separating Persons from Ideas
1995

"You need to earn more!" Phoebe said, scowling at the pile of bills.

"How?" I said, putting on my backpack.

"Figure it out," she said as I walked out the apartment door.

Living off a $12,000 per year stipend was economically hard, even for a single person. I knew I needed to make more just to cover the rising costs of rent, food, and utilities. Meanwhile, Phoebe bought lots of personal belongings: shoes, dresses, art supplies, and jewelry. She also enjoyed going to concerts and out to eat.

Writing is tough business, I thought, as I followed the campus path from the Shakespeare Garden to the Searle Student Center. The beauty of the campus grounds, trees, and brick and stone buildings no longer seduced me.

The hard economics of writing had overshadowed the lure of material beauty. Most of the time, I wrote for three cents per word. The average story I sold was about 2,000 words or $60! I had made a whopping $750 over a six-year period where I had written, not published, over one million words according to my documents' word count.

I ordered a huge plate of rice for three bucks, the best deal around, to fill me up outside Ramen noodles, and I sat to eat on a bench under a tree overlooking the manmade inlet pond.

Academia seemed to be a dead end. Even my advisor told me that if he had to do it again today, he would not be a research scientist. Less than three percent of grants were getting funded, meaning only those with a track record of publications had a fighting chance of getting grants renewed.

Yes, occasionally a rare young academic would win a young investigator's award and break into the publishing ranks, but I did not see that happening to me. I would need another path.

I tossed the empty plastic plate and plastic fork in the garbage and started my trek back to the tech building.

Technical and medical writing paid better. I had made $20 per hour as a technical editor, and medical writing was all the rage back then when I could earn up to one dollar per word on a radiology paper as a ghostwriter. As a subcontracted medical science writer, I freelanced and made maybe a few thousand each year. Perhaps I would launch my own business?

The 'how,' though, was a big question. I had energy, enthusiasm, tons of ideas, but I did not know how to get started. Did I try to get a powerful career job in pharmaceuticals to amass wealth and power?

How? I was raised in ignorant poverty, I didn't even know how to write a resume.

Phoebe was a talented artist and was able to find gainful employment in graphic arts. So, she was earning some money, but her spend rate was higher than her earning rate. I wondered how I would fare trying to replace her biological father as her sugar daddy in the future, if I stayed with her.

Phoebe's Dad would send her money when market gains permitted. I did respect his earning ability. Also, he did have some level of faith, although I never figured out just what he believed. Phoebe's dad supported her, her brother and sister, her cousins, and he was a generous man. I gave him that.

The problem was that Phoebe had a spending habit that I could not afford, nor did I know that I ever could afford. If I did earn more, would she just spend even more, always outspending our current income and leaving us in permanent debt? Even as a graduate student, as a couple, we were already over $44,000 in debt.

****

On my walk from Searle back to the tech building, I saw a group of students in white shirts waving banners off the left of the path. One flew a kite. Another blew bubbles. Two were tossing a Frisbee back and forth. The one thing in common among the group was that they were energetic and happy.

I could have easily passed by them unnoticed, but instead I walked up to them.

"Here," a young brunette said, "have a pamphlet."

"Thanks," I said, looking it over. "What are Christians for Christ?"

"We're a campus movement to tell people about Jesus."

"Why do that?"

"What do you want out of life?" she asked.

"I need to earn more," I said.

"Money is not the answer," she said. "Many have nothing other than Jesus but are joyful."

"I want to fit in," I said.

"Join the wedding feast!" she said.

"Wedding feast?" I asked. I wanted their social connectedness, but not the 'magic' faith.

She laughed innocently, "Jesus will help you fit in."

I paused. The hardest thing for me was separating the image of my human father from my Heavenly Father in my mind, so even if there was a God, I hated him. "Is it possible to fit in by seeing religion as a philosophical way of life while leaving God out of picture?"

"There is beauty that cannot be seen," she said, raising her arms and pointing to the people and trees.

"Your words and actions only have meaning in relation to how they affect people," I said.

She put her arms down. "How odd you are. Won't you give Jesus a try?"

"I'm okay with god as a distant idea, perhaps a higher power that started the wheels turning, but then left mankind to his own devices and abandoned us."

"Jesus lives in our hearts," she placed her hands on her chest.

I walked away, but I was impressed by her joyfulness. I wanted that interior joy myself and wondered if I could have a community like that without the faith component. In discovering that logical, successful people were religious, I had to give up the idea that logic would lead all people to atheism. In fact, I had to admit that at least at a social level, religion made logical sense.

****

After doing some research, I convinced Phoebe to come with me to the Baha'i Temple in a nearby town.

"Wouldn't it be good to find like-minded people?" I asked her as I parked the car.

We walked up the giant steps.

"I'm only going this one time," she said, as I helped open the solid doors for her.

The Baha'i Temple was a giant dome wrapped two-thirds of the way around by Sheridan Road on a small hill. Lake Michigan could be seen from the steps of the northeast face of the dome.

"Wow," I said, lifting my head and staring at the large, near-empty building.

She shrugged her shoulders.

The inside was mostly empty, with people milling about glancing up and down and around them. Near one entranceway was a small table with brochures. I picked up a brochure and scanned it. The Baha'i Temple was supposedly a combination of the world's seven great religions. Nonetheless, the interior was a round barn shape with nothing to focus on as my eyes swam along the perimeter.

As my eyes scanned the perimeter, there was periodically a short statement on the wall such as "no alcohol," "no pork," etc. There was one "no" for each of the world's seven great religions to combine them all together and appeal to all. To do this, it occurred to me that most of the doctrines had to be removed, or debased, to their simplest form.

In the end, it seemed to be a philosophy about almost nothing at all. However, people were here in a community of sorts, and I imagined they could rely on each other to a certain extent. This was an improvement over thinking that I could do it all on my own. I needed a small group who thought as I did, a community that attempted to serve the common good in the sense understood by humanists.

I glanced at Phoebe and could see that she was bored, so we left.

"It's nice," I said, half-heartedly. I studied the blank barn room one more time and wondered where God was in the emptiness.

"Yeah," she said, "but we are not going there again."

I paused, then shook my head.

So, I snuck out, to go there again.

****

"Let's just stay in tonight," Phoebe said.

"But the neighbors invited us to a party; don't you want to go?" I asked.

"Please just stay here; we'll watch this movie and be together."

"We can do that anytime. Don't you think it would be rude to ignore our neighbor's invitation?" I implored.

"No, it would be rude for you to leave me here alone," she pushed the VHS into the video slot.

"I have to go. I already RSVP'd. What do you want me to tell them about your absence?"

"Whatever," she turned away, making herself comfortable on the couch and patting the spot next to her.

"Come on, what are you doing?" I pleaded.

She walked to the kitchen entrance. "Hiding the knives."

What?! I thought, *why*? I stood upright as my shoulders became a ridged beam. "I'm going now, see you later."

She waved goodbye, "All we need is each other."

"Yeah, but my friends, they have this joy, don't we want that?"

"No," she said, "I do not."

"Why not?" I asked.

"Happiness is not how you amass power. Power is gained by manipulation. So, there is no need for happiness, which is just an emotion."

"I want to see my friends," I said, putting on my coat.

"But why?" she pleaded.

"I want more ideas, more opinions, more options."

"More than what I can give you?" she asked.

I could not answer her, but yes, I wanted more than even my words described. *Did I want a magical god*?

She waited, arms folded.

"You are cheating on me," she said soon afterwards.

"No!" I said, but deep down I felt that I was cheating because, while I was not cheating with another woman, I was cheating with a new idea.

****

There were so many beautiful things in this world. I lay on the couch remembering the trees swaying in the sunset from the night before. There were so many beautiful people. I thought of the young women and men at the church on Sunday. They seemed full of joy and what they had in common was that they were believers.

"Stop daydreaming," Phoebe said.

I sighed and came back down to earth, to the apartment, and looked at her.

"How did your meeting go with Dr. Choan?" she asked.

"He will not allow me to progress any faster through my doctoral program."

"Hmph!" Phoebe said, folding her arms. "Well, I am going to defecate in an envelope and mail it to him."

My eyes widened. I started to laugh, but when she did not join me, I stopped. That did not sound beautiful to a humanist.

"How will that help my graduate degree? I'm not following this."

"The curse will get him to do what we want for you." She said, folding her arms and stomping away on high heels.

Phoebe had other ideas about how to behave that I did not agree with, but that I permitted. She wanted to harm other people, get voodoo dolls, and use curses upon anyone who got in her way, or my way, she would take care of. I wish I had been in a better position to help her to see the error of her ways, but I was not.

When she wanted to harm friends and family, I became concerned. I was a very logical person pursuing a PhD in a science. I couldn't help but wonder whether in time, she would do the same to me.

Would the wolves eventually eat each other if there was no one else left around to attack?

Chapter 15
Wolves Devour Each Other
1996

"You know, after mating the black widow spider kills and eats her lover," Phoebe said flatly.

"Yeah," I said. "So?" I shrugged, but I remembered the spider and spiderweb I saw with my sister Judith and the lesson of death. My eyelashes flickered rapidly.

She ladled a thick stew into my bowl.

I ate immediately, despite steam wisps fogging up my glasses. The soup was rich with noodles, chicken, and green leaves that were so salty, yet smooth. I could not stop eating those green leaves. I pointed to the bowl. "What are they?"

"Just something I whipped up for you," she said.

"Wow, thanks, they are soooo good!"

"That's why I put so many in there for you." She smiled, sitting, and sipping from her tea cup.

I devoured three bowls and moved to the couch.

"Wow, great soup!" I said, leaning back on the couch pillow.

"Yep," she put the dirty dishes in the sink, then looked back at me. "Need a drink?"

"Well," I said, "now that you mention it, I am pretty thirsty."

She brought me a tall glass of water.

I chugged it down and handed it back to her. "Another, please."

She filled it again and I drank it. We repeated these three more times. The fifth drink spilled down my shirt. I squinted at her.

"Maybe you are allergic to herbs?" she offered, smiling.

"Maybe," I said, laying on the couch and drifting off to sleep.

****

Happy, shining people walked along the Lakeshore Drive.

"Wow, so many people!" I said.

"Yeah," Phoebe said, "but it is hot out here."

"Oh, yeah. I'll get us drinks." I walked to the vendor stand.

"Hurry up," she sat on a rock in some shade.

"The largest size please," I said.

"That'll be $8.00."

"Jeez, I only have a $5.00" I looked behind me at Phoebe. "I need three dollars."

She grunted, opened her purse, and stretched out her hands to give me three crisp bills.

"Thanks, here," I handed them to the vendor, along with my crumpled five. I gave the drink to Phoebe.

"This'll do," she said, adding sarcastically, "How long would you last without a drink?"

"Let's go see the skyline. It's just a little further."

"Just a little further? I've heard that one before." She looked around. "I'm going to the restroom."

"All right. I'll wait here," I said, my eyes searching for some shade. After she left, I sat on the same rock in the shade. I imagined the taste of the frozen lemonade. They were pricey but were the best thirst quencher in the blazing heat.

The crowds walked by, every type and shape of person. I people-watched as if I were studying the social animal and searching for the best specimens to study.

The sun had shifted. I walked north on the bike path. I saw a group of green port-a-potties. *She must be in one of those.* So, I sat under a tree in the shade, but I was still sweating profusely. Pooosh, a green door opened, a big guy came out. *Poosh, nope, not her. Poosh, nope. No. no. no. Maybe she walked south?*

I wandered south, slower now, past the vendor, down the path, around a bend, to another beachfront with changing rooms and real bathrooms. I sat outside the women's bathroom, feeling like a jerk watching beautiful young, fit, women wait in line and others coming out. I stretched my neck each time a woman came out, hoping it would be her. *Nope, not her.* No. No. No. One woman glared at me.

"Sorry," I mumbled, "I'm just waiting for somebody." I turned away.

I ventured north, further then last time. Ugh. Back south, faster now, further than before, past the beach house, to see the skyline but not see it at all.

The shadows lengthened. I checked my wallet again, no cash. Now what? All I had left was my CTA card, a ride, and a transfer left.

Each step felt like I was walking in molten lead. I could barely move. What if she was lost, kidnapped, or dehydrated? Wait, she had a frosty lemonade, so she should be hydrated. But what if a bad guy got her? My heart pounded. My shirt, shorts, and socks were drenched.

I saw the sign for the Fullerton elevated train stop. I pulled out my CTA card and slid it through the slot, bumped through the turnstile and up to the platform, leaning heavily on the railing.

A train pulled in. I got on. The train moved. I sat down and stared at the map. *Uh-oh! It was a Ravenswood train. Wait, I could go to Pat's place.* Then I would have help finding her. The train moved along, swaying side to side, clunking on wooden rails, until the Montrose stop.

I got off, ran down the stairs, sprinted to Chris' place, pushed the button, and he buzzed me in. It was a race to get to his apartment before the buzzer turned off. Pat opened the door.

"Mooooo with it!" Pat mooed.

"Hey, Moo-man!"

I jumped into their apartment and sat at the kitchen table, "Hey, Crystal."

"Hey, Paul, this is a surprise! What brings you here?"

"I lost Phoebe," I said meekly.

"What?" Crystal said. "How? Where?"

"Bike path on Lake Shore Drive. I'm worried she's in trouble!"

"Naw, Moo-man," Pat chuckled. "Did you try calling your apartment phone?"

"No, but that's a good idea."

Crystal handed me their phone. I called.

"Hello?" It was her.

"What happened?" I asked.

"I went home."

"Huh? Why?" I sat down.

"You seemed fine on your own," she said slowly, "in... the... heat."

"I'll be home when I get there." I hung up.

"She's there." Crystal laughed.

"Here, man, you need a drink." Pat handed me a

Leinenkugel's glass bottle.

"Thanks, man," I twisted off the top and chugged it down, "but I can only stay a little while so the transfer is still valid on the card."

"That gives you an hour," Crystal said.

"Come on out on the porch," Pat led me to the fanned porch. "We'll catch up."

"Nah, man, another time. I've got to get back."

I finished the drink, then headed out. I got on the train again heading south, transferred at Belmont to the red line going north, and transferred at Howard. The train moved like a turtle. Every time it stopped, I swore under my breath. I got off at Noyes, ran to the apartment building, and unlocked the hall door, the front door.

There she sat on the couch, reading *Glamour* magazine, sipping on a soda.

"Well," she said, "here you are, again." She sighed.

Nothing she said after that made any sense to me. What? Why? How? No answers were clear at all. It was a mystery that I still do not understand to this day.

****

There was such overwhelming beauty everywhere around me: wind, fruit, the scent of sweet flowers, sunshine, and beaches full of sands of red, black volcanic rock, yellow, pure white, and other mixed colors.

"Try these flippers," Phoebe said, smiling.

"Cool," I grabbed the flippers and stretched them onto my feet. I'd never tried flippers so thought it would be fun. I ran to the waves and jumped in.

Splash! The waves pulled me out. I tried swimming strokes but still was pulled out. I started breast stroking and was able to stay in the same place, fighting the undertow.

Wait! I remembered I had flippers on. I pushed off with the flippers and pressed towards shore. I raised one arm up to try to get Phoebe's attention.

She sat on the towel, about 150 feet up the beach, and waved back to me.

No, I need help! I paddled, breast stroke, flipper pushed, felt sand under my knees. I tried to get up onto my knees. I waved her towards me again.

She smiled.

A wave knocked me onto my face, sand went up my nose, and saltwater was in my mouth and in my eyes. I got one knee under me and pulled the other knee to the right of me in a triangle motion. I squatted, raised both arms, and waved to her frantically.

She smiled and waved back with both hands.

Ugh, I went under again. Blub, blub, sand, salt, blah! I pulled up on my arms, arching my spine backwards. My head above water, I inhaled. Another wave was coming, held breath, under again, looking at sand cloud.

I twisted on my side to face up towards the sunlight. I paddled with the flippers and felt the back of my head grazing sand. Another couple strokes; my chest was above water. I flipped over again, pushed off the sand with my arms, got up onto my knees, and tried to bring one foot under me. Splash. I was back under water.

Gurgling. Each time I tried to stand up on the flippers, I fell again. Instead of trying to get up while still in the water, I needed to lurch out of the water almost completely.

I pushed up, air again, breathed, under again, twisting to see light. Backstroked, paddled flippers, pushed, paddled, dolphin stroked. There was sand on the back of my head, but not good enough. Paddle, backstroke, again, again, pushing my head into the sand, head above water, chest above water. Pushed, paddled, back stroked again. My thighs were above water.

Movement stopped. I tried to paddle, stroke—nothing. I was beached. I rolled over up onto my knees. I pushed off to carefully get one foot on sand, then the other foot. I was upright. I tried to catch my breath. I walked directly to her. My legs and arms were scuffed up with sand, reminding me of the rug burns my dad gave me.

She smiled.

"Couldn't you see I needed help?" I cried in a weak voice.

"Well, you are here again, aren't you?"

****

"So, she hid the knives again," I said. My clothes were badly wrinkled. I tried to flatten my shirt with my hand, but to no avail.

"Why?" Antonio said.

"I think she's mad about my having friends," I offered.

"That is not a reason to hide the knives on you," Antonio stopped moving, and stared at me, making eye contact. "I think she is trying to get rid of you."

"What do you mean?" I laughed.

"Come on, man! Think about the four stories you've just told me."

"Coincidence," I said. I smelled sweet perfume. Antonio's wife Dalisay was walking in, I could always smell her rose perfume as she arrived.

"You should move out," she said.

"Huh?" I replied faintly.

"You really should end it, Paul," Antonio affirmed her words.

I sat down and placed my right hand on my forehead. "Isn't that a little extreme?"

Antonio sat to the right of me. Dalisay held his hand. "You do not belong with this woman. She's no good for you. Don't you know that we don't like her?"

"Oh," I said. I got up and started to walk away.

"Come over to our place for the next Bulls' playoff game?" Antonio asked.

"Yeah," I waved behind my head, "I will."

"Don't bring anyone," Dalisay shouted behind me. "We have some friends you should meet."

I turned my head, "No pressure?" I smirked.

"She means my brothers will be there from Italy, that's all," Antonio offered.

I smiled, waved, and returned home.

****

"We never go anywhere!" Phoebe said, pouting.

"Where do you want to go?" I asked.

"Somewhere normal people go, like Disney World, skiing ..." she said.

"But we went to Disney World last year," I reminded her.

"That did not count! You played Elric with your friend. We only went to Disney World at the last minute," she retorted.

"Okay, you want to go skiing?"

"Yes," she said.

"Fine, but where do we get the money to go?" I asked.

"Don't worry about that. My 'normal' family will pay our way."

We met her family at a courtyard outside a government building. I was shivering. As they spoke to each other, I watched puffs of air jump off their faces.

"Ice cream!" Phoebe exclaimed.

They walked over to a street vendor stand, and I followed.

"Here you go," she said, smiling and handing me a big bowl of ice cream.

"Thanks," I replied meekly.

Phoebe and her family ate from their one-scoop cones, watching me to see what I would do. I scooped out a spoon of ice cream and ate. It was good. Phoebe smiled again. I shivered, inside and out.

Next, we were in a Jeep with chain wheels driving a steep road along the foothills of a huge cone-shaped mountain. Phoebe and her family chatted excitedly about the trip. When we reached the top, they seamlessly put on their skis. My hands shook as I tried to tighten the strings and close the straps. I'd never skied, yet no one offered to help.

Then we were outside, and they were ahead of me. I tilted my skis, so I could walk like a bowlegged duck as they became smaller ahead of me. Finally, they were like ants climbing onto a lift. I hopped on the next lift, gripping the metal railing tightly. The carriage lurched off the ground and swung back and forth. I searched ahead for them. I thought I saw them getting off at the top of the peak. When I had arrived, they had already gone down and come back up the steepest slope.

"Hurry up," Phoebe shouted back to me.

I jumped off at the end and stood on shaky legs. Then I duck-walked to the steep peak. I looked down at the 45-degree angle which must have been a few thousand feet down. I jammed my ski poles into the snow hard. I bent my knees to stay very still. People were screaming and laughing and talking. Every few seconds, I heard a "whoosh!" as someone would fly by me.

"Move over!" said a man.

"Oh, sorry," I replied, duck-walking to the left side of the top where the line was forming.

My heart pounded as I stared down the slope to spot Phoebe and her family. I was drenched in my own perspiration. My undergarments had been sticking to my skin and now the cold wind was freezing my wet skin.

Whoosh! A boy flew by me, down on his knees with his head tucked in. *Wow, he moved as fast as an arrow.* Then a couple went down the slopes, side by side, swaying one way and then the other. I tried to move my arms and knees to imitate them, but kept my poles jammed into the ice so as not to move an inch. A family went by together. Was that them? No, wrong-colored snowsuits. I looked down at the snow and tried to breathe slowly, listening to the sounds of happy voices around me.

"There you are!" called Phoebe.

I turned toward the sound. She was halfway down, ski-walking up along the side of the slope.

"Have you been down yet?" She eyed me up and down, red-faced.

I shook my head no.

"This is ridiculous!" She glanced behind her. "Dad, Paul is too afraid to ski down the slope!"

"Is he now?" her dad yelled up to her and me.

My cheeks grew flush. I leaned backward and nearly let my bottom touch the ground. Then I crab-walked the ski poles to slowly go down the hill in a "z" pattern.

Phoebe and her dad watched me for a while, then exchanged glances, smiled, and resumed climbing back up and skiing down the steep slope.

"Whoosh!" Her brother flew by my right side. Snow pellets plastered my face.

I felt imbalanced and pushed both ski poles into the ground to my left to stay upright. Then, I crab-crawled down the hill, watching the sun sink into the west. As I neared the bottom of the high summit, huge snowflakes hit my face. Soon there was a white cloud around me as snow came tumbling down. People were muttering and heading for the ski lift to take them back down.

I watched Phoebe and her family get on a carriage and head down, so I duck-walked to the lift and followed them back down.

On the way down, my shivers increased. I could not feel my hands or feet. I felt water sliding down my front and back sides. My legs were stiff, and my knees were a little swollen. I felt dizzy and closed my eyes. I could not wait to be on flat ground again. The ski lifts lurched, and I slid away from the lift down to flat ground. I allowed myself to fall back onto the soft snow and gazed up at the snowflakes as they danced down to my face. The earth was still and flat against my back. I smiled.

"Hurry up!" Phoebe said.

I sat up. Phoebe and her family were already in the Jeep and were staring at me. Her mother shook her head.

"Come on!" said her dad.

I pulled myself up with the ski poles. I duck-walked to a bench, took off the skis and boots and placed them, along with the poles, in the rental return baskets. Facing down, I trudged to the Jeep and got in the back seat.

"Hmph!" Phoebe turned away.

I was silent. She touched the back of her hand to my head. "You are burning up." She smiled, teeth showing.

I remember very little of the ride after that. Soon, I was in an ice bath at a hospital. Two short men in white gowns wearing surgical masks and latex gloves wrapped around their wrists were talking to each other at the foot of the hospital bed.

"Hypothermia?" I heard the one wearing the stethoscope say. Then he made eye contact with me. "No, he has a 104-degree fever."

"It looks like Vietnamese-Russian pig flu," murmured the other gowned man.

The two exchanged glances and then came to my bedside. The first said, "I'm Doctor Ruthmeier." He pointed to the second, "And this is Doctor Watiski."

"Now think," stated Dr. Ruthmeier. "Have you been near any pig farms?"

"No."

The two men looked again at each other.

"Has your immune system been compromised

recently, heavy drinking, staying out late at night ...?" asked Dr. Watiski.

I shook my head, recalling the image of myself standing outside eating ice cream and struggling to ski on my own for the first time.

"Well," Dr. Ruthmeier started, "you'll be in medical isolation for the next seven days."

I scanned all around me and saw white bands of cloth in the air above me and to the sides of me. There must have been something metal holding it together because there was plastic covering the whole bed like a dome.

"How long have I been here?" I said, seeing the news on the television on mute in the corner of the room.

"Three days," one nurse answered.

Three days? Day and night blurred. Eventually, I was moved to a regular hospital bed. I heard a slight movement in my room. Startled, I woke up.

"You still here?" Phoebe sighed in disgust as she sat in a chair, studying me. "Don't worry, my family has taken care of the hospital bill."

"Oh," I said. "What happens now?"

"You get released and we go home," she replied. "How could I know you were this frail?" She shrugged.

****

"I need to go home to my parents for a while," Phoebe started.

"Why?" I asked.

"I need to refill my gas tank," she said, smiling.

"Well," I said, thinking I could work on my doctoral thesis, "maybe a little time away would be good for both of us. I could work on my dissertation, and you could 'fill your gas tank.'"

Phoebe hugged me, but I just stood there. She called her parents and arranged a flight to her parents' home.

We were at the airport. We went to a coffee stand, got coffee, and sat and made small talk. She checked her watch. "Time to go," Phoebe said.

"So soon?" I asked.

"I need time to get through security," she said neatly.

We hugged. I followed her to the security line. She smiled and waved back.

I paced back and forth behind the line as if I were a puppy watching its master leave for work. I craned my neck to see her head. I walked back and forth faster. She turned back once more and smiled. Phoebe's teeth flashed. She watched me panicking, and she liked it?

Phoebe then disappeared through the gates. I paced back and forth faster, then stood still. I stared at the blank spot where her head had just been. I was frozen for a while, then I turned around and made my way through the airport corridors back to the train station.

That night, I lay in bed. The apartment was silent. The silence frightened me. I held a pillow tight to my chest. I stared at her empty side of the bed. I arranged a line of pillows where she would be laying. I turned toward the pillows, spooning them. It did not help. I knew they were pillows. Then, I turned away from them, holding a pillow in my hands. I tossed and turned again and again. I glanced at the clock. It was 2:03 a.m. in the early morning. I got up and went to the kitchen fridge. I took out the half-gallon of orange juice and poured a glass.

I'll be fine, I thought. *She'll be back in a week.*

Ten days later, I got a letter in the mail. The return address was Phoebe's parents' address, written in her handwriting. I ripped open the letter.

"Dear Paul: I need to stay longer at my parents' house. I'm having a good time sleeping in my bed, seeing my high school friends, and eating all the local food I grew up with here. You will be fine as you have your dissertation to keep you busy."

Would I be fine? I had lost a few pounds already. My hands shook. I was unable to read anything more. Did it end with I love you? Probably, but I was having a hard time believing those words right at that moment.

I buried myself in my doctorial lab work, but even doing that, there were many hours left to be alone, think about her, and miss her.

Twenty days later, I forgot to pack lunch again. I pulled up my loose pants, put on my blue lab coat and set about getting beakers and flasks out of the lab cabinets. My lab coat fell loosely around me as if I were a scarecrow. I had lost over 20 pounds.

I had thirty minutes before I needed to lyophilize the white product powder I hoped to see in small specs. Even a few specs were a good yield, enough to run my experiments for a couple weeks, but I had to watch every minute to get a good yield.

I sat at my lab desk, next to the post-doc. She wrote feverishly in her lab notebook. I imitated her and wrote up my notes as best I could, but I knew I was nowhere near writing the quality of her notebook. My hand shook, and I dropped my pen. As I reached down for it, my sleeve went up my arm exposing my thin white wrists.

Karen beat me to it and picked up my pen for me.

I accepted the pen, "Thank you." I had learned not to bug Karen. She was a much better scientist than I was and was determined to follow her husband Bob to the pharmaceutical industry.

She studied me up and down. "When was the last time you ate a full meal?" Karen asked. "When does Phoebe come back?"

I shrugged my shoulders.

"This is ridiculous," she said, leaning to get her lunch freezer pack. "Here," she handed me a heavy-laden plastic box. "Bob made me extra stir fry; you can have it."

"Thanks," I said, accepting it, "maybe later." I got up to go to the lunch room.

Karen leaned towards me as I stood up and we accidently brushed hands. We both froze for a moment. The warmth of human touch felt alien to me.

Karen sighed, "You need to call Phoebe and tell her to come home to you."

I nodded, left the lab and put the food in the lunchroom fridge.

"When?" I implored speaking into the phone.

"I'm still not sure," Phoebe replied through the phone line.

"I feel weird," I said, shaking, "like I'm slowly dying."

It sounded like she was going to vomit at my weakness. "Really," she stated, "and how long *would* it take you to die?"

"I'm not sure...maybe several weeks? I'm having trouble remembering to eat." I said scientifically, forgetting that I was discussing my own mortality. "So when are you coming back?"

"Hmph," she said, "I'll let you know."

"I love you," I started to say as the line went dead.

"Are you going to the movies?" Delilah asked.

I stared at my worn-out sneakers. "I don't know if I should." I was just numb all over.

"Don't worry," she said, "we're just friends."

"I trust *you*," I looked up, "just not so much me. Phoebe has been away over five weeks now."

"Nothing will happen," she laughed. "Why are you with her anyway?"

"I'm more *not* with her recently..." I fumbled my words, "I love her?"

"You are asking me?" Delilah snickered. "I'll see you at the movies."

I did go with her and her Christian friends. The movie was dumb, and I wanted to leave, but it was better than sitting alone in my apartment for another Saturday night.

"Thanks for inviting me," I waved as they dropped me off.

"God is looking out for you!" Delilah called back. I could see the reflection from the golden cross hanging from her necklace.

God? I sneered to myself.

I unlocked my apartment door and there I was, again: alone. Alone, in uncomfortable silence.

My weight kept dropping each day, I had started to welcome the possibility of death when ...

"Surprise!" Phoebe announced her entry two weeks later.

I hugged her tightly.

"Okay," she said, "let me get my coat off first."

I backed away a few steps. "What made you decide to come back?" I asked.

"My dad was tired of me lying around the house," she laughed, "and he said I should go back to you."

It was not the answer I was looking for.

She eyed me up and down. "You lost weight," she said, adding, "I'll cook something up. What do we have here?" Phoebe walked to the kitchen and peered into the cabinets and then in the fridge. "Nearly empty. When was the last time you went grocery shopping?"

I shrugged. "I made friends while you were gone."

She slammed the fridge door closed.

"What *sort* of friends?" she asked quickly.

"Just friends," I answered.

"So, I'm not enough?" She folded her arms.

"No, you are..." I rubbed her curved arms, "...*great*." My voice dropped off; I doubted my own words.

Phoebe titled her head. "Women friends?"

"Two are women."

"Two?" she said, mouth gaping open.

"They are just friends; most of them are guys."

"You were hanging out with two single women while I went home?"

"It was no big deal," I replied. "They are just friends who worship their God."

"Christian women?" She stomped her foot. "Why did you not tell me this on the phone?"

"I don't know."

"Just great," she said.

Chapter 16
Seeking God
1997

"I should kill Dr. Choan!" Phoebe blurted out.

"No!" I shouted.

Things between Phoebe and I were going from bad to worse. She was losing patience with the time it was taking for me to finish my PhD. I needed to find a "real" job. I didn't want to lose her.

She was startled.

"I'll talk to Dr. Choan," I whispered.

"Is there any way that I can speed up the doctoral process?" I asked my advisor.

Dr. Choan paused, then said, "There are a number of control experiments that need to happen to make sure the protein effect is real."

"I understand that," I said, "but could I do it on an accelerated timeframe?"

"Science cannot be rushed," my advisor said.

The assistant to the professor spoke up at that moment. "Dr. Choan, you've got to let Paul go."

Dr. Choan shook his head, no.

I left his office, shaking. I had to find a way to make this work.

****

"We can get you in front of three firms in one trip," said Joe on the phone to me.

"That's great!" I replied, adding "when?"

"How soon can you get out to New Jersey?" he asked. "It is the pharmaceutical capital of the world. You will be set for life once you settle in there."

"I plan to visit my family in upstate New York in July," I replied.

"Perfect," he said. "Just pray."

"Pray?" I asked.

"Pray to Jesus! Ask Him to be your Lord and Savior," the recruiter said.

I was so sick of him talking about Jesus, but I really had no answer to his statement and did not want to offend the one person who was getting me job interviews.

Once I went through the interviews, I was offered a job as a medical writer. It was a foot in the door of the lucrative career I wanted, and Phoebe demanded money to support her high-flying lifestyle.

****

"I'll be living in New Jersey and commuting back here to finish all the control experiments." I told my advisor. "I'll keep writing my dissertation and defend it in front of my committee in December."

"I don't think this is a good idea," said Dr. Choan.

"I have to do this for Phoebe," I replied, and quickly left his office.

****

"I'll FedEx you the contract. Read it over, sign it, and return it," Joe said.

Phoebe was already packing, and my friends came over for a goodbye party. We got on a plane and started our new life on the east coast.

****

The panels and overhead compartments shook above me. *Would I ever get used to this airplane commute from Evanston, Illinois to Princeton, New Jersey*?

I landed, and an old limo driver picked me up with my name on a sign. On Mondays, I went straight to the office from the airport. The hustle and bustle of busy young professionals met my entrance. I sat at my desk. Taylor came in first.

"How was your weekend?" he asked.

"Frantic," I said, rummaging through office papers.

"So, are you going to stay here or move back there?"

"I don't know." I kept working, so Taylor left.

Peg was next. "You know, Paul, my husband left me just like your dad left your mom."

"Yes," I said, "you told me."

"And, I do not want you to end up acting like your dad."

"Acting like my dad? What do you mean?" I was shocked anyone would compare me to him.

"You said he started riding a motorcycle, left your mom, and now lives with a nurse."

"Yeah," I said, "so, I am not doing any of those things."

"But you are getting your own interests away from Phoebe."

I stared at Peg. It was true that I was making new friends, some were women, and some were men. The commonality between them was they were Christians, seemed happy, and lived better lives than I did. I was unsure of what to say.

"Your woman should come first," Peg said.

The women in the hall must have overheard us. They chanted in a you go girl spirit: "Uh-huh, that is right!"

I fell silent. What do you say to the relationship cheerleaders when you live with ... with an enemy?

****

In New Jersey, God put many more Christians in my path.

Ryan Droupper, Harvard M.D., fellow medical writer, laughed at my atheism. "Turn to Jesus with your problems," he said.

I really admired Ryan for his writing ability, his wit, charm, laughter, good nature, and his intellect. I was puzzled that he attended the Church of Christ.

"Why don't you join me for Sunday service?" he asked.

"I'd have to sneak out to do it," I said.

"Then sneak out!" he told me.

I laughed and politely declined his invitation, although the offer stayed in the back of my mind.

****

After a few months as a medical writer, I decided it was time to take the next step in my career, so I began searching for higher level opportunities.

It was during this time that I had my mysterious car accident. My car spun around while other cars were not affected. I landed in a ditch, got out in mud dirtying my suit, and asked a farmer for help. He told me God would bring help. I scoffed, wondering how such impractical advice could be given to a potentially injured me. To my surprise, a tow truck arrived. I watched traffic whiz by and no one stopped, noticed the accident or slid at all.

I sat in the front seat of the tow truck and we drove to a repair shop. The car was fine.

I called the human resources person at the pharma company. She told me to go to the hospital to check for injuries. I arrogantly insisted on going ahead with the interview. Imagine a guy with a mud-covered suit going into an interview in a hospital-sterile office building.

I did not get the job, of course.

After my botched interview, I went to see a doctor who determined I had a concussion and needed some rest.

I took a few days off.

Unfortunately, both Ryan and I ended up being laid off as medical writers. He was much less devastated than I was and repeated his offer to have me attend church with him.

The Sunday after being let go, Ryan brought me as a willing guest to his local Church of Christ service.

The church was a big, round building with little decoration on the outside or inside. In this sense, it reminded me of the Bahai temple. So, I proceeded in my faith-walk where I had left off but this time in a Christian church.

As Ryan and I entered the church, people greeted us with big smiles and shook our hands.

Then the minister started suddenly, "Jesus is our savior." Reverend Dan spoke for about 25 minutes, offering ideas, thoughts, good feelings, and a few corny jokes.

Okay, I thought, *that is nice, but so what*?

Then wheat bread squares were passed around. The bread squares were not introduced in anyway. I remembered the Eucharist as a child, but was this the same?

Ryan ate one, so I ate one. It was nothing, just stale bread.

Afterwards, a smiling young woman in jeans carrying a guitar came over to us.

"Paul," said Ryan, "this is Kelly. She runs the young adult group."

We said hello and then Kelly introduced me to several young adults in their twenties and early thirties. They were so friendly and happy. Just standing there, they were happy.

But ... but why were they happy?

****

Ryan was happy. I wanted that.

He dealt well with pressure. I wanted that too.

Perhaps if God existed, I was not on my own. I met wonderful people at the Church of Christ. I was overwhelmed by their happiness and friendliness. I am still grateful to these Christians even many years later for their witness of Christ.

They introduced me to mere Christianity, not only with love but also with knowledge. They could describe to me why they were Christian and what it was about being Christian that made them different. I wanted that. I quickly joined their church and started to slowly begin to believe that Ryan might be right.

Ryan got me an appointment with the minister to help me with my career angst.

I liked Reverend Dan and was grateful for his advice. He helped me separate out my fear of my biological father from the eternal goodness of God. Given my father was my first example of a father, all I knew was my dad's agnostic preaching and poor fathering skills. I can remember my father talking to me maybe ten times in my entire childhood. I had depended on him for leadership and it was not there, so I assumed there was no leader at all.

The minister helped me understand that God is real and is an adopted father to all of us; we are all His adopted children.

"God walks with you," Rev. Dan told me, "and carried you when you were at your weakest."

I became okay with a distant unobtrusive God with a capital G that did what I wanted. In other words, I thought the relationship was that when I want something, I would tell God what to do for me. Kinda like a spoiled kid, was I.

When I didn't have an immediate need, God went away. This level of understanding I call the "God sword" level: when I need God, I summon him, and He does what I want and then goes away. The God sword requires no code of conduct on my part. In this sense, it is not a god at all, but a magic wand, a milk-and-cookies God who did what I wanted.

I imagined, as perhaps many do, that so long as I did not hurt anyone else in an obvious manner, and at the same time, I was doing good things, that therefore I was good overall, like the TV hit "The Good Place." I had a blind eye to anything that potentially may have hurt others or me, or my relationship with a real God.

Chapter 17
Milk-and-Cookies God
1998, Princeton, NJ

Reverend Dan taught me a lot about the Christian faith. He was an excellent teacher and patient with my questions. As a scientist, I was trained to dig deeper and deeper. Many have since called me a doctor of questions. I believe pressing the limits of what is known is everyone's duty. Eventually, I did wear on him. Rev. Dan did a lot for me, but then I noticed some limits to his patience and knowledge.

I sat down with Reverend Dan a final time to try to get to the roots of my questions. We discussed the Golden Rule: *'Do unto others as you would have them do unto you.'*

"But the Golden Rule is *not* in the bible," I said, since Reverend Dan claimed that the bible was the only as a source of revelation, but where in the bible does it say that the bible is the only source?

"Yes, but the verses suggest the Golden Rule," he replied.

That was strange, I thought. That meant there were mental exercises, sources, people external to the bible that decided what the bible meant.

"Well, then suppose that I liked beating myself, would that mean I could beat others?" I asked.

"No, uh, natural laws would say not to do that," he said.

"Whose natural laws?"

"God's natural laws," said Reverend Dan.

"But who is interpreting them?"

"Well, we each can have our own personal interpretation."

I paused. "Doesn't that get confusing?" I asked.

"How?"

"People may not agree with each other and how then do we decide who is right?"

"I look to known evangelists for answers. I see what they have to say."

"So, there are a body of people whose interpretations are considered right?" I asked excitedly.

"Well, you can pick the authorities who agree with you," Reverend Dan capitulated.

My eyes widened. Reverend Dan shattered my growing belief in a truth.

"So, then, each person is right, and can find evidence to support their own ideas?"

"Yeah," he said, rubbing his chin, and pausing a moment.

"What's wrong?" I asked.

"Well, I was just thinking. I'm twice divorced, and I wonder who God would say is my wife?"

Wait, he did not know? I was silent for a minute. "Are you asking me?"

He shook his head. "I suppose it would be the first wife."

"According to whom?" I whispered.

"Some of the best Christian thinkers," he pointed to his overstuffed bookshelf.

"Some? So, there are others who do not agree?"

"Yep, some say it is the second, or the current wife that God would call your wife." Reverend Dan threw his hands up into the air.

"*You* do not know? How can that be?" I was flabbergasted.

"God is sometimes such an abstract concept that it is okay to develop a philosophy and then decide what is right for me."

That disturbed me. Reverend Dan seemed to be switching between a real God with a capital "G" and an imaginary god with a lower case "g," whenever it suited his position.

"Would you use that idea to pick a surgeon?" I asked.

"No, I would find out who is the best."

"Why not do that with religion; find out which one is the best?" I asked.

Reverend Dan did not answer. We just sat there looking at each other for a while.

I saw him as a student of faith, ahead of me, but much like myself. Reverend Dan no longer appeared to be a valid source of truth to me. That was because he told me there was no one he could go to for true answers.

I thought this was sad.

In science, there are authorities even amongst experts.

Certainly, Reverend Dan knew more than I did, but still seemed to have an incomplete belief. He had helped me a great deal, counseling me one-on-one and instructing me in the basic tenets of Christianity, but I still had questions.

Was there a true faith that stood out from other faiths?

Was there a place that I could find the answers that I needed?

****

In my class on the great world religions, I found the Christian faith puzzling because it did not make immediate totalitarian sense to me. I could see how other religions could be made up, but not Christianity, which seemed strange and alien to me.

I began to feel uncomfortable with Reverend Dan's advice, which in many ways was like the advice I had been given by the secular counselor I had in college.

Was this all there was to life and God, just secular relativism, where 'I'm okay, you're okay,' et cetera?

It also bothered me to find out the preacher had no one to go to with his problems. He was his own authority, or as I thought, he was his own god, and a poor god at that.

Two weeks later, I felt empty as I continued to go to the Church of Christ. This emptiness reminded me of the sadness I had felt after partying.

I mean, the congregation at the church were nice, shook hands, hugged me, gave me milk and cookies, and made me feel good. However, I found myself looking around the building of their church and wondered as I had before in the Baha'i temple:

Where, in here, is God?

****

"Where were you?" Phoebe asked, scowling, when I got home late one day.

"At the library, researching jobs," I lied. There were many times I was at the local library doing just that, but not this time. I was attending service at the Church of Christ.

"No, you were not!" Phoebe glued her eyes to mine. "The library is closed on Sunday."

I was silent. I folded my arms and leaned against the wall.

"You are cheating on me!" Phoebe accused.

"No." I denied it weakly, but in a way, I *did* feel I was cheating on her. The Christian way of believing and living was very far away from where we were as a couple.

"You are!" she said.

We stared at each other, neither one willing to give ground on their position, both seeing the other as a liar. Both of us were right

We were both liars.

My girlfriend found out I was sneaking out to be with other people, but she did not know they were Christians. Eventually, she realized what I was doing.

"You are not going to that church," Phoebe mandated. "If you become a Christian, you will eventually become a Catholic, and I will not have that!"

I was silent but kept going to church.

And then suddenly my life changed again.

My girlfriend found out and she left me.

I became very depressed about her leaving.

"You okay?" Kelly from the Church of Christ asked me over the phone.

"Yeah," I said, my voice shaking.

"There is a group at the church you can join for support."

"No thanks," I said. I had a feeling I would not be going back to that church again.

The doorbell rang.

My mom and sister Judith came in. They helped me clear the kitchen sink out. They helped me set up a place to eat in the back. When my mom saw the empty bedroom, she cried. I did not know what to say. I barely understood the situation myself. We ate on the back patio.

I cried.

My mom held me.

Judith watched us and then made tea.

****

"Why don't you commit suicide?" Phoebe asked.

I hung up, as if the phone had transformed into a living tarantula. So, that is what she wanted? Or is that what the devil wanted through her?

Phoebe's uncle had recently committed suicide. When she described his suicide to me, she said it in a matter-of-fact manner. "His life was no longer meaningful, so he committed suicide."

No longer meaningful to *whom*? I imagined it had some meaning to her uncle, and those who cared about him.

The prowling lion came to me in dreams, circling, hungry, and ready to pounce but for a white sphere of light, my guardian angel.

What did the evil one want of me?

It wanted me dead, wrists slit, fallen several stories off a building, my guts spilled out, my bones broken apart, my dead eyes staring up at the sky, and my body writhing in an agonizing death. I would become food for worms, to quote Shakespeare, and a lost soul for eternal torture by his minions in hell if I took my own life.

"Jesus, Jesus, Jesus," I repeated three times, my hands clasped together in prayer. The horror scene of my own suicide faded into white light, gone from my memory.

That was what Satan wanted of me, dead, a slave forever in hell.

Perhaps Phoebe did not realize that, as she still did not acknowledge the existence of Satan and hell, but it was true, whether she understood it, or not.

"I miss you," she said the next time she called.

Really? I thought. For several months now, Phoebe had belittled me with words over the phone.

"You have been telling lies about me to my family and friends behind my back. This is over! Do not speak to my family or me again!" I hung up the phone.

Phoebe always had told me I needed to learn to defend myself, and so I finally had, but little did she know that God would help me defend myself, from her.

The phone rang again.

"But I said that I missed you," Phoebe cried out.

"Do you forgive me?" I asked.

"No," she said in a puzzled voice.

"Do you admit to doing anything wrong?" I whispered.

"No."

"Will you allow me to be Catholic?" I asked.

"No," I heard her foot stamp down on the floor.

I paused. *Catholic*? Surely, I meant to say Christian.

"It is over," I said, hanging up the phone.

The phone rang again.

I ignored it. Instead, I closed my eyes, praying, trying to forgive and forget her. If I spoke to her any further, knowing her denouncements of faith, I would be handing Phoebe the power to destroy me. "The devil is but a barking dog on a leash," my sister Pam had told me. "It can only bite you if you walk towards it."

The phone continued to ring.

My left arm reached for it, but my right arm held it back.

I prayed some more.

Eventually, the phone stopped ringing.

The apartment was silent. For the first time in many years, I did not fear the silence. Instead, I welcomed it.

Chapter 18
Truth Thrust Upon Me
1999, Chicago, IL

The very next week, I found myself walking into a Catholic church. Mass was being celebrated and I took a seat in the back. I stared at the crucifix and the tabernacle and remember thinking and sensing somehow, like a sixth sense, *here is God*!

The priest said with great strength, "Lift your hearts up to the Lord!"

I gazed at the crucifix, and tears poured down my face.

After Mass, I went right to the confessional and gave my general confession.

"Father, it has been more than *10 years* since my last confession at Confirmation…" and then it poured out, all my sins I could remember. I cried, words sputtering between tears.

The priest laid his hands on my head, walked me through the Act of Contrition, and gave me absolution.

In that very moment when the priest touched my head, I believed on faith that it was the Catholic Church that I needed.

"Yes, you should return to the Catholic Church," the priest told me.

"On what authority does the church act?" I asked him.

"On Christ, who founded His Church in Peter."

Finally, someone had pointed to an authority to understand truth.

I walked out on cloud nine, feeling a hundred pounds

lighter. I was overjoyed at being clean, feeling as light and white as snow. I really do not understand how so suddenly my heart warmed and I converted.

Suddenly, I was Catholic.

I still do not understand that.

I believed that many must have prayed for me. I thanked them in my heart.

****

When I considered my life and others' lives, I saw joy and pleasure, but also pain and suffering. Real life includes pain and suffering. Here, before my mind and in my heart, was the only faith that understood pain and suffering.

The Protestant ideas of 'happy, happy, joy, joy, milk and cookies' just did not match the real human experience. So, I never returned to the Church of Christ. It was hard, but it was doable. I found myself making a lot of hard decisions like this that I was too afraid to make before.

The moment I walked out of that confessional, I was filled with an indescribable joy. I loved everyone, especially my enemies. I forgave my father and Phoebe. It would take me a long time to catch up to that logical decision on a human level, but I was amazed I could even take the first step of forgiveness. It was as if my prior problematic black and white Charlie Chaplin filmette version of reality was replaced with new 4-d plasma screen technicolor glasses that graced me suddenly to see the reality that was real.

Here is an analogy I've used to describe how it is all worth it to be Catholic.

In the Old Testament, Satan was permitted to afflict

Job with loss of farm animals, crops, family, friends, farm land, wealth, and gives him boils, et cetera, to test Job to see if he would still love God. While he grumbled and complained, ultimately Job passed the test and still loved God.

So, a man feels like Job. Things in life are just not going his way.

So, he prays to God and says, "God, I do not get it. I go to Mass, Confession, give to the poor, do whatever I can to help others, and still things are not going my way. If only I could ask you some questions?"

So, a voice booms down from the Heavens and says, "Shoot! Fire away with your questions."

"God, is it true that you are all powerful and can do all things?"

"Yes," boomed God, "it is true."

"God, is it also true that you stand outside of time; that to you a million years is but a second?"

God says "Yes, that is also true."

So, the man says, "God, would you do something for me?"

God says, "Anything, just name it."

And so, the man says, "Would you get me a million dollars?"

"Sure," God replied, "Give me a second…"

I tell this story because no matter how smart we think we are, no matter what universities we attended, what jobs we have had, or how famous or important we think we are, it does not matter because each one of us is a flawed human who will never even get anywhere near the intellect, power or abilities of God.

Never are any of us, including Lucifer, in any position

to outmaneuver God, ever, in any way. We should approach God in fear and trembling as we cannot compare ourselves to our Creator, God. And when hearing God's Truth, should we not give up everything for God's Truth, the treasure of great price?

I felt filled with grace, and I was ready to face a reality of pain and suffering for the promise of eternal joy. And it did not take long at all to feel the pains of loss. I quickly lost my friends, family members, peers, professional colleagues, atheist friends, agnostic friends—even the friends I had made at the Baha'i Temple and Church of Christ—once I resumed the practice of my Catholic faith.

My atheistic and agnostic friends said I had become Catholic because of my car accident and the concussion, but that was not the case.

I think there were a series of events over several years that were pulling and drawing me, like a metal droplet to a mega-magnet drawing me to this God (with a capital G) by His (with a capital H) Truth (with a capital T). And most of that time, I was clinging to my own sins to prevent being drawn in. Also, I was medically cleared of the concussion within a few days of the car accident, and yet, I was still Catholic. Might Jesus have used the concussion to be the great surgeon of the mind and aid in my conversion? Maybe, could be, for I had no rational explanation for my moment of conversion.

I am still grateful to this day to those Christians and people of faith who led me to God's Truth. However, once I had discovered the True Church founded by the Christ, there was no going back without lying to myself. There was no going back to any lesser, or partial, truths.

Only in the Catholic Church, had I found the treasure of great price, and I was ready to sell everything I had to gain that wonderful joyful treasure: Truth with a capital T, Love with a capital L, the Way with a capital W. The beauty and joy of God's Truth still overwhelms me with joy to this day.

Life is still hard from time to time, but I know that I can choose each day to pick up my cross and follow Christ carrying his Cross on his way to Calvary. I know that I can offer up my pain and suffering to Jesus, and He will make good use of it. God can take what is broken and fix it. Christ is the great surgeon of the mind, the great freer of the soul, by forgiving our sins when we ask with contrite humility in proper form to be forgiven.

Despite all the pain, the suffering, the loss that I experienced when reverting to the Catholic faith, it was well worth it, and I would do it again 7 times 77 times, even in the face of tragic social losses. True Catholicism is a narrow road, and not an easy road, but a road well worth the journey to get to know, love, and serve Jesus, and to enter into His Father's Joy in Heaven.

I had found something so much greater than the sum of all other things that I had ever experienced that I wanted to be the smallest servant in the eyes of the great God.

I offered up my pain and suffering and losses to Christ at Calvary on His Cross, and many times I recount the Christ, the Great Surgeon of the Mind, healing me of spiritual and mental wounds.

On a logical level, I forgave and loved everyone,

prayed for my enemies, but the emotional ability to forgive and love my enemies only came to me over time by the grace of God.

Sometimes, I trembled in Joy because I had heard and began to know Truth and I wanted that, and only that. Knowing that Truth as an adult in good conscience, who would not want the Truth?

Chapter 19
Voracious Appetite for Truth
2000

Questions remained in my head, but now that I was sure God existed and that His Truth was in the Catholic Church, I had faith that all my questions would be answered. For the most part, they have been answered. Some questions, like how to explain the Trinity, or the mind of God, are still a mystery to me; and in the gap between ignorance and knowledge resides faith.

As it is said, reason is the wings on which faith soars, and so I soared.

I returned to the Catholic priest and asked him many questions. He was able to answer all my questions; I wondered if perhaps he was just very clever. He gave me some books to read.

One was the *Catechism of the Catholic Church.* I spent an entire day and night reading the *Catechism* in one sitting. Afterwards, I was in awe of the *Catechism* as a rational, logical guide. I could see no flaw or point to attack. Here were the instructions on how to live! In this book, I saw a perfect guide for how to live one's life in holiness and joy, despite what happened around me.

So, despite my personal circumstances, I had a great joy in the knowledge that Truth existed and that I had had an opportunity to know Truth.

I had always wanted the best: the best science program, the best novelist, the best mentor, the best way to live, and now I had found it. I had found Truth.

Of course, one of the responsibilities of knowing

Truth exists, and beginning to study Truth, is that there is no way of going back. As a result, I lost a lot of friends, became alienated from some family members.

Like I said, science colleagues assumed I had gone crazy: I got a concussion and went insane. Of course, they were wrong. The concussion was long gone, and I held down a tough job. I was rational and Catholic at the same time.

I needed a way to survive the social castration I faced. The answer came to me in a dream. I stood on the top of a flagpole. My bare feet barely fit on the ball top. As I looked below, I could see the top of a tower several hundred feet below me. Below that was the ground. There was a light breeze and I was cold.

Fog rolled in.

I knew immediately that I could not sustain my balance alone in such precarious circumstances. I prayed to God for strength. I felt the presence of the Holy Spirit; Grace came down upon me.

I remained perfectly still, like a statue glued to the flagpole.

There came high winds; still I remained.

There came rain; still I did not move.

Thick black clouds covered the skies above me. Lightning flashed. Crack! A second later thunder smashed the silence; still I remained.

Light snow started to fall. It covered my feet, shoulders, and head in a white blanket. Then the snow thickened. Still I remained.

God preserved me. There must have been a reason I still lived, but why?

In reading the *Catechism* all in one day, attending Mass, receiving the Eucharist, and making frequent confessions, I was beginning to gain True knowledge about God through closeness to His Church.

As I attended Confession more frequently, I began seeing more and more of my sins. It was no longer enough to me that I did not kill, rape or steal, but I then noticed venial sin and actions I had assumed were good, but had bad consequences to my relationship with God, others, or myself.

Reading *The Imitation of Christ* by Thomas á Kempis also helped me see that many times when we think we are helping others, we are hurting them. The passage "Take the log out of one's own eye, before attempting to take the splinter out of another eye," really struck home for me.

As I spoke to Protestants and cafeteria Catholics, I realized this barrier was a big issue for so many. The assumption that if I mean well, then I do good, is as flawed as mankind is sinful. We cannot measure ourselves against criminal minds. We can't measure ourselves against our peers or ourselves. We must measure ourselves against God, who is perfect. And in that measure, we are always coming up short and in need of His Church to redeem us.

Jesus told us, "Be perfect, as My Heavenly Father is perfect." But we cannot achieve perfection without the Grace of God through the Christ and His Church.

Yet, even in this turmoil of my new awareness of my faults and failings, I felt great joy because I knew that Truth exists, that Truth has been revealed, and that Truth can be known, and that eternal paradise is reachable to all.

So, at this point I was beginning to get to know God, but I was still too immature to love and serve Him.

****

I had additional questions that were eventually all addressed in RCIA back in Chicago after receiving my doctoral degree. For example, I did not understand Mary's role, yet at the same time I accepted that I would eventually understand. The faith was in me, part of who I had become, and I could see I was already a better person, more concerned with others, as though scales had been removed from my eyes.

The world looked and felt different, more real, and I wanted that more and more. I began going to daily Mass, praying the Rosary every day, reading the Bible cover to cover. I was voraciously hungry for the Truth now that I knew there was a Truth with a capital T.

Knowing that there is an absolute Truth, I had to follow God into the Catholic Church. There was no going back to a little "t" truth of convenience. I also accepted that the pope must be the head and authority along with the bishops of the body of the Catholic Church. For the Christ identified Peter as the first pope. "You are Peter, the rock, and on this rock, I will build my Church… and not even the gates of hell will prevail against it."

As a Protestant friend from the working world said to me, "I'm jealous of you Catholics because you just follow what the Church tells you, while we Protestants have to guess."

So, I turned to him and said, "Then join us, come into the wedding feast." And eventually, he did! That was a great moment where the Holy Spirit directed me to convert another soul for God.

While everything Protestant sounds nice how can one

both protest and love God at the same time?

There's a contradiction.

These attempts to Protestantize the Catholic church are been easily resisted throughout the over 2,000 years of Catholic history.

In the past, saints lived a clearly Catholic life. Looking at the history of Christianity explains why major contemporary Protestant seminaries often lose whoever teaches the history of the Church because that history of Church teacher ends up converting to Catholicism. A good source of this is the Acton Institute of Ethics and Economics in Grand Rapids Michigan.

Then there is the denial that Jesus is God *and* man. We all believe historical figures based purely on whatever written information we have on them. For example, we believe that the Caesars existed because we have written documents about the Caesars of Rome.

The best historically documented figure is Jesus Christ. So, based not only on what He said, but also on what other said about Him, you should arrive at one of three conclusions:

One. He's a liar and anybody following him is also a liar. Historical evidence simply does not follow this logic.

Two. He's just crazy and anybody who follows him is just following a lunatic. Once again, there's no historical documents to suggest he's not sane.

Three. He is who he says: He is the son of God.

This is the toughest one of all because if that's true, then we really are facing an absolute truth outside ourselves. This is the most terrifying one for people. Because it implies that we would have to change our lives by love of God before ourselves and love of our neighbor before ourselves to reach the pearly gates of Heaven.

The evidence supports this hypothesis. For example, the apostles were willing to die for the beliefs that Jesus imparted on them. Would they really be willing to die for Jesus if he were a liar or insane?

Also, think about who surrounded Christ and the apostles and their followers? The Jews and the Romans, both of whom, for different reasons, wanted to disprove the Christian claim that Jesus rose from the dead. Would not the Jews or Romans have shown Jesus remains, even his bones to prove he was dead? Since no one has found the body of Christ, did he die and remain dead?

No.

Finally, think of the apostles. The words, actions, and miracles of Jesus impacted them all enough to die for what they believed. Would any gang, cult or organization really do that if its members knew it were fake?

No.

So, logically, it must be real. Jesus is who He said He is: the Son of the living God, the only person and God in history to raise Himself from the dead.

Some will still not accept this and will instead endlessly demand evidence. The doubting Thomas who demanded that he would not believe Christ unless he put his fingers into the holes in Christ's body. Christ resurrected and came to Thomas, so that Thomas could put his fingers through the holes in his body. He said to him: "Blessed are those who have not seen but have believed."

****

"So, that is why white lies are okay." Professor Burns stated. The professor of Business Ethics at the Ross School of Business at the University of Michigan at Ann Arbor received his Doctor of Jurisprudence from Notre Dame, considered by many to be the most ethical law school in the United States

"Sorry, why again is that?" I asked.

"Well, Paul," he said, leaning against the chalk board, "let me tell you a story and you decide, okay?"

"Okay."

"My relatives and I had gathered around my grandmother's bed. Prior to going in her room, the oncologist, Dr. Renquest, had met us in the hall to let us know Grandma had maybe three to four weeks left to live.

"'Three to four weeks to live!' I had said to the doctor. 'This is only October and her favorite holiday is Christmas and she will not live to see it?' Dr. Renquest nodded. Well, just then Dr. Renquest peaked his head in the door. 'Mrs. Burns, we need to prep you for your follow-up infusion.' My grandma asked him point blank, 'Dr. Renquest, will I live to see Christmas?' My family and I turned to the doctor, with pleading eyes. 'Yes,' he lied, 'you will.' And that was the kindest white lie ever told," concluded Professor Burns.

"But..." I started.

"No buts about it. There is a time and a place to discreetly lie a little bit." He retorted.

"But the doctor did not lie," I said.

"How's that?" said Dr. Burns, shaking his head.

"For those in union with God, for those in the afterlife, they are more alive in eternity than we can understand." I blurted out.

"Huh? Catholic theology. Well, you, Paul, are the most difficult student I've ever begrudgingly given an 'A' to."

The class burst out laughing and applauded. I felt that they laughed at me and applauded the professor. I wondered if Dr. Burns' grandmother could see us. If she were in heaven, could she go anywhere, at any time and even be watching us at that moment? As for me, I was becoming more comfortable with publicly sharing my faith, but there is always a price to be paid for Truth. I believed it is worth the price of public betrayals. Christ had Judas, and in a way, we all do as well.

I studied my classmates' faces. A few had neither laughed nor applauded. They appeared to be thinking. And all thought is dangerous to the nonbelievers because all roads lead to God. "Seek and you will find. Knock, and the door will be opened for you."

Chapter 20
Catholic on Wall Street
2001

Just prior to the recent millennium, I was single with no girlfriend, living chastely, like a monk, in a small apartment. I continued to read, pray, and serve as an usher at my local parish in Chicago. As my faith continued to grow, I had more and more opportunities to share my faith with others.

In fact, *Time* magazine ran a piece on my parish that offered the Latin Rite Mass. I was interviewed as a PhD scientist from a prestigious graduate school who was Catholic and attended Latin Mass. Unfortunately, *Time* can have a liberal bias and they chopped up my words, making me look like a fanatic, which I am not.

Then, as a still-forming Catholic, I suddenly found myself in a very ethically challenging environment when I was recruited to be a Wall Street analyst. I thank God that I was Catholic by that time.

While still a student of the Catholic faith, I was well on the way and so was able to resist several temptations on Wall Street that otherwise surely would have compromised my soul and perhaps would have otherwise landed me in jail.

The platform of power my ex-girlfriend Phoebe had wanted me to obtain was suddenly upon me, and I did not want it.

I reacted the exact opposite way I had thought I would when I reached the platform. There are a lot of good people trying hard to do good on Wall Street.

Nonetheless, ethical perils are common daily occurrences there.

When people ask me to explain, I tell them there are several categories of players who make up Wall Street: traders, sales people, bankers, analysts, portfolio managers, etc. Each player has a goal and there is nothing wrong with each goal in and of itself. The problem arises when those players are placed in the same room. For each player's goal to occur, someone must take, and someone must give, and that is where ethical conflicts arise. The Wall Street analyst, rating stocks and industries in company and industry reports, sits in the middle of the spider web.

One theme in my life is that I always wanted good information. When I chose to be a scientist, I wanted the best program. As a religious person, I wanted the best belief, the Truth. As a Wall Street analyst, I wanted the best information, but even then, it was difficult to obtain it. Businesses and industries hide information. I wanted to help the average person on the street, but my role was not geared for, or permitted, to do that.

****

Two years later, I met my wife Mona, who was on her own revert path to the Catholic Faith. I brought her to my parish and our betrothal began. We became engaged and remained chaste throughout our engagement.

The Catholic Diocese of Chicago, under Cardinal Francis George, had a new premarital program called FOCUS, which asked each of us over 200 questions and then compared our answers. The purpose was not to decide if we should marry as discernment of the marriage vocation was another part of the marital program. Instead, the goal of FOCUS was to help those intent on marriage to be prepared to handle differences and build on our similarities. It allowed us to be prepared for emergency situations and have a plan of action. For example, how do we handle guests upset at the wedding, or what do we do in the future if we have kids and a drunk uncle wants to spend the night recouping at our house, etc.

FOCUS solidified my faith as I realized I would never know how to handle these situations on my own of my own inherent ability, but that with God, anything is possible. At a minimum, Mona and I had a plan for when the storm would inevitably rock our marriage boat.

My wife was also a Wall Street analyst. We each were on our path to being stronger Catholics and pulled each other along the narrow path. We agreed at a certain point we would leave Wall Street. My wife left Wall Street when our first son was born. No one believed I would leave. "Paul, nobody leaves Wall Street but in a body bag." Heart attacks were common and, unfortunately, I did see people leave that way.

When we reached our agreed-upon financial goal, I left too.

I believed that if I did not leave soon, I would give in to temptation. I made a promise to my wife and I wanted to keep that promise. However, that alone was not enough to help me leave. The longer I was in that environment, the more intense the pressure became. I am not invincible. I started having nightmares where I would wake up in cold sweats. I felt I could not live with this anymore; luckily the timing was right, and I left.

The ability to leave Wall Street was a grace from God. I do not believe that I was strong enough to leave simply because I made a promise to my wife; I needed God's Divine intervention.

When I left, I did not want to continue to help big hedge funds and mutual funds get richer; I wanted to help average people with their investments.

So, I started helping individuals on the retail financial services side. I knew that the average person had poor information. When I would go to a hedge fund or mutual fund and meet with an industry portfolio manager, I would pitch them with my stock ideas. They would shake their heads and then show me information that I did not have, surveys, etc.

It occurred to me, in a sad way, that if I did not have the information, even after accessing public information and doing tons of hard fundamental research, that there was no way the average person could compete with big funds.

The lack of fairness made me reflect on the universality of the Catholic Church, where the Mass is the same Mass anywhere in the world and the *Catechism* is the same *Catechism* anywhere in the world. In science and on Wall Street, I had witnessed injustice, but the Catholic Church presented the true justice of God and His Mercy, and I liked that justice and mercy. In getting to know God, I could not help but love God. In getting to love God, I could not help but want to serve Him. I wanted to create a little justice in my own way by helping teachers, non-teachers, Catholics, and non-Catholics understand rewards and risks to avoid making major financial mistakes.

I prayed daily for God's help to make my family's life

a domestic church. I wanted them to know God, love God, and serve God. I wanted to help my family and others make it to Heaven by creating a 'domestic church' where we all can flourish. Since then, I have slowly built my own financial consulting firm, and designed it so I could put God and my family first. Putting the interests of my God, my wife and children first meant putting my career second. Also, I put the interests of my clients ahead of my interests, as any good fiduciary ought. After knowing, loving and serving God, I had to put serving my neighbor ahead of serving myself.

And who is my neighbor?

Everyone is, according to Christ.

Chapter 21
Cast Out into the Unknown
2004

"That's it?" I said to Colleen, our realtor. She had called with an offer on our house which we had been trying to sell for five years.

"Yes, while it is a lower number than we had hoped for, at least it's a sale."

"Yeah, it is a sale," Mona sighed.

"I just feel the house is worth more than that!" I said excitedly.

"I agree," said the realtor.

"We have to think this over," said Mona.

We hung up the phone.

"I love this house," I said.

"Me too," Mona replied.

Mona and I exchanged glances. Then we hugged.

"What should we do?" I asked her.

"Well, right now it is time for dinner," Mona said. "Anyway, we have a few days to think it over."

We ate silently, occasionally asking the kids about how their day went. After cleaning the dishes, we spoke again on it.

"What will we gain by moving again?" Mona asked.

"A better school district," I started, "but, several retired teacher clients of mine have told me that more taxes and better school budgets do not automatically mean a better education."

"It certainly does not mean better formation," Mona added.

"True," I whispered. "Why don't we at least look at our local parish school?"

Mona smiled and nodded.

"Kids?" I yelled.

"They're in the basement," Mona reminded me.

We walked down the stairs to the source of so many noises.

"Kids," I said again. "How would you like to go to school at your parish?"

Their eyes widened. They shouted, "Yeah!" and they jumped up and down.

Saturday, we were in our local Catholic school lobby.

"We love big families and can offer free uniforms for all your kids," Principal Don stated.

The kids started trying them on from a clothes rack. I touched one of the uniform pants. Immediately the memories of St. Martha's Catholic School in first grade came back to me. I went to public school except for that moment. Now as an adult, I had taught at Catholic School, and in my heart of hearts, I wanted our six children to go to Catholic School.

"Please, let's sit down with our marketing director Sally and our priest, Father William," he said.

"Sure," Mona said, corralling the kids to a big table in the principal's office.

"Give your money to your local parish, not higher taxes to the local government," Father William said, maintaining a big grin.

Don and Sally handed us the marketing and application packet and sent us home smiling.

That night, I prayed to God, "Please help me know which way to go: move to a better town with a better school district, or stay here and send the kids to Catholic school?"

I did not hear an answer in my heart and fell asleep precariously.

Sunday, I awoke to a cup of coffee on my bed stand.

"Thanks, honey," I whispered, sipping the coffee. I dressed and went downstairs to the living room.

The Sunday paper was on my coffee stand next to my wingback chair. I read the front section, same old, same old: so many deaths, so many thefts, a sports game coming up … until I turned over the front section to the back page.

There was a full-page ad spread that started "In God We Trust." Below that were quotes from America's founding fathers, presidents, Supreme Court justices, congress and leaders in education and foreign policy.

"Huh?" I said aloud as I read the full page. The quotes seemed to be stating the reasons that God is a central part of our Judeo-Christian heritage as a nation, but it was something else that caught my attention. Hand to God, three times I read words that led me to consider our local parish in that advertisement.

"We're staying and sending the kids to Catholic School," I stated to Mona.

"Thank God," she replied, sipping her coffee, "You finally caught up to me."

"How can I compete?" I laughed, saying in honor of Mona, "A good woman's intuition has a direct line to God."

And so, we did. We stayed and sent our kids to our local parish school. And so goes the irony of man's plans, we turned down the offer to sell the house and instead followed God's greater plan.

Mona and I have had six children in 15 years. We have been blessed with a beautiful family, a nice home in quiet suburban Chicago, and a burgeoning career for me. She and I have weathered the marriage storms well, through good and bad times, in prayer, staying close to the sacraments, faith, hope and love, especially the greatest of these, Love.

As my faith has taught me to let go and let God take the lead, my life has become more of a mystery and less in my control. I do not often know what my schedule will look like for a day or a week coming up until it happens. There are many great fruits once someone lets go of the reigns of control to God. I thank Mona and my sisters for introducing me to St. Therese, the Little Flower, and her little way of humility. God knows better than I do how to be good, endure trials, and be joyful.

****

I have been a fan of *The Journey Home* show on EWTN television station since 1997. As I mentioned, I first had the pleasure to meet Marcus Grodi in 2006 when I brought my wife and the three children, we had then to EWTN to watch live shows including *the Journey Home*. How I ended up there is an amazing story in its own right. At that time, I asked Marcus how one gets on his show and he said that if I wanted to be considered as a prospective guest on the show that I should write my conversion story and send it to him at the coming home network. Ten years later, on January 10, 2016, I was the guest on *The Journey Home*.

I did not realize the effect that episode would have on my family, myself, and those who watched it. I am grateful to God for the opportunity to share my story. Many people have contacted me: some with questions about faith; some who want my help with their financial matters; and some who are discerning their vocations, whether consecrated layperson, religious, or married. Besides helping the average person, I also pray for other families to create a good domestic church for their family to flourish and be formed.

Chapter 22
Evangelization at Work
2007

I have known my atheist friend Pat since we were undergraduates. It has amazed me that despite our changes in careers, jobs, lifestyle, family life, religion, and philosophy that we have somehow remained friends. Recently, he watched the YouTube video of my *Journey Home* episode. He started calling and visiting me, peppering me with questions about the faith. I was so glad to see him Catholic-curious.

"God, if he exists, is evil!" Pat exclaimed, leaning back in his metal chair, looking skyward.

"How do you come to that conclusion?" I asked.

"Well, there is evil in the world, so God is evil," he concluded, sighed, and sipped his coffee.

"Evil exists, can we agree on that?"

"Yep," he said, taking another sip of his coffee.

"Imagine a God who loves us," I offered.

"Okay."

"Imagine that He loves us so much that He gives us free will."

"Free will?"

"To do as we choose."

"Oh," said Pat, "yeah, so."

"God also loves us so much, that despite His knowing we are better off loving Him back, but He permits us to choose not to love Him," I said.

"Hmph," Pat sighed.

"And in choosing not to love Him, we sin and out of sin, evil consequences arise."

"So, we are back to evil in the world. God could just stop it," he rallied.

"Yes, but He chooses not to, just as he allowed Adam and Eve to commit original sin at the beginning of human history."

"So basically, he is letting us fail?" he asked.

"Yes, but He sent His Son with a way to help us back to God."

"I have done so many things wrong," Pat acknowledged.

"That's okay. God made a sacrament to forgive our sins."

He got up. That was all he was ready for at that moment. I did wonder, though, was it possible that I was the only person he knew who could help him come to God? I think we all must ask ourselves the price of not speaking the Truth and choose to speak Truth with love and firmness whenever possible.

****

"Hello?" I answered the phone.

"Hey Dr. Paul, this is Arnold."

"Sorry. Arnold who?"

"Arnold Fezzer."

"Arny? From Wall Street?"

"Yes, it's me. I just watched your *Journey Home* and heard you on Relevant Radio."

"Oh?" I asked.

"Yes, and guess what?"

"I have no idea," I said.

"I'm Catholic now."

I was silent.

"I converted to the Catholic faith."

My jaw dropped. “Arny, that is wonderful. Congratulations!”

“Yes, I went into rehab after leaving Wall Street and now I’m Catholic and praying and loving it!”

“Wow,” was all I could say.

After the call, I sat on a box in my garage, manning our annual garage sale.

“What’s wrong, dear?” my wife asked as she was unloading the minivan on the side street.

“You will never guess who just called me to tell me he is now Catholic?”

“Probably a buddy from Wall Street?” she asked.

“Good guess; how did you know?”

“Because you look so shocked.”

We laughed.

“Yeah, not only that, but this guy was among those I would have least likely considered one to convert!”

“Amen,” she said, handing me a bag of groceries.

The conversion of Arnold Fezzer from arrogant alcoholic to humble Catholic blew my mind. Surely, I am but a seed, and God is the one who grows the plant and allows the soul to flower. This was something I had never imagined or dreamed, and it happened right before me.

****

There is also the question of how to bring those partly in the Church into the fullness of the Church. Here is one conversation I had with a Protestant woman friend.

“Imagine that you were diagnosed with terminal cancer and had one year to live. What would you leave your children to remember how you taught them Christianity?” I asked.

"Instructions on how to live well," replied Debra after a pause.

"Great; what form would those instructions take?" I asked.

"Written," she replied, confident that the analogy was the Bible as she had a Bible-only and faith-alone-saving mentality.

"Okay, and how would you make sure that they understood your intentions in the writings correctly?" I said.

"My husband would help them understand."

"And how would he do that?" I asked.

"By explaining it to them, by watching over them, and protecting them."

"I see, so that would take actions on his part?"

"Yes," she said.

"So, besides the written, there is the verbal and the actions?"

"Yeah, so?"

"Verbal is traditions and actions are deeds," I said.

"My faith is simple; I follow the Bible and I do not need tradition or deeds."

I was tempted to point out that she just now said she did, but I decided to let her figure that out. "Suppose a man were ill and he decided he does not need a doctor?"

"He needs a doctor." Debra had been a nurse.

"Right, but he does not think he does. Our ideas can be wrong. Truth is a real, absolute standard. Of course, a sick man needs a doctor. People are sick with sin and need God as He established salvation through His Church that Jesus founded."

We chatted on about other matters. I knew Debra's

limit had been reached, for now. God would do the rest. He always does.

****

"Our Protestant church is based on tolerance," said my older friend Bob.

"Tolerance of what?" I asked. I respected Bob and needed to tread lightly.

"Of people and who they are," Bob said.

"And who are they?" I asked.

"They are the variety, the plurality of humans expressing themselves as individuals."

"We Catholics would call that the dignity of the person, that each person is made in the likeness and image of God, and therefore, has intrinsic value regardless of how society values them," I said.

"I would not go that far," Bob said. "If someone is no longer serving a purpose, they can choose to die."

"Kill themselves?" I asked. "Help me understand your position. Do you mean they can euthanize, commit suicide, or murder others?"

"Well, no, not murder," Bob said.

"Which one is murder: abortion, euthanasia, first-degree murder?"

"Only the last," Bob stated.

"So, you are making up rules," I said.

"No, just common sense, is all," he replied. "Women have the right to choose."

"To choose to murder?" I asked.

"Not murder, just part of her body." Bob stated.

"Scientifically, we know each cell in the fetus is not the mom or dad, but a new person."

"Still not murder," he repeated.

"So, the fetus is alive and then after abortion it is dead. The old so-called useless person is alive until euthanized and then dead. But these acts are not murder?" I asked.

"No, they are necessary small wrongdoings."

"Small wrongdoings?" I whispered, "They were alive and then are dead."

"Enough of that. I know you have a Catholic agenda," he said.

"Just expressing the natural law, is all. These ideas are not uniquely Catholic as there are Jews for Life, Muslims for Life, even Atheists for Life."

"Still, you are Catholic," he stated.

"I am," I said, "and you are in a Protestant church built on tolerance. I simply asked what you are tolerant of?"

"But I answered that." Bob stated.

I tried a different angle. "Are you tolerant of Catholic social teaching?" I asked.

"Only if it is not in our church," he scolded me, raising his finger, then he restrained himself and laughed.

"So then, your church is not tolerant of the over one-billion Catholics, one-sixth the population of the earth?"

"We decide what to tolerate," Bob said, biting his muffin.

"Yes, and what not to tolerate?" I asked.

"Uh-huh," he said, wiping his mouth.

"So, you have a yardstick measure for tolerance, and I have a football field measure for tolerance?"

"Something like that," he said.

"And who is to decide whose measure of tolerance is correct?"

"Both are correct, yours for you, and mine for me," he said, proudly folding his arms.

"But our measures are different, and only one can be right. They cannot both be right at the same time."

"Why not?"

"Well, let us look at abortion. Either the result is a dead baby or not."

"A dead pile of flesh," he concluded.

"So, we ask scientists and they tell us…"

"…it is a dead blob of flesh."

"No, they tell us the moment that egg, and sperm unite, that even that one single cell is a unique person."

"Maybe," he said.

"No maybe about it. Look at the genes, half mom and half dad, but combined uniquely and entirely unrepeated in the universe."

"What about twins," he asked.

"Yes, twins' genes can be same or almost the same, but the expression of those genes varies and continues to vary their entire lifespan. Also, they have free will and can make different choices and are different people."

"Say anything you like, it is still a pile of flesh."

"You and I are a pile of flesh then?" I asked.

"Yes, but we function…"

"As we are meant to function. So, does a fetus function as it is meant to function?"

"Nah," he said.

"Look to what the first *Californian Medical Journal* had to say about how an aborted fetus is not a human. They essentially state even though it is medically a living person, that to accomplish a social agenda it must not be, and so words can be used to make it not alive."

"So?"

"They altered what they knew to be true to get the result they wanted: more sex with supposedly less consequences, but not really," I said.

"End justifies means," he said.

"It leads to unjust war, if I want your land and property and resources."

"There are justified wars."

"Yes, rarely," I said, "but we are getting away from the point. They lied."

"So, they lied." He capitulated, thinking little of it.

"You agree then?"

"Yes, they lied. Why are you smiling?" Bob leaned in towards me.

"If we agree they lied, that means we agree by analogy that there is truth."

"I know where this goes; you want truth with a capital T."

"Yes, an absolute Truth with a capital 'T' that is not relative, not dependent on what you or I or anyone want to believe is true with a little t."

"How inconvenient," he said.

"How so?"

"If there is an absolute truth, then I would have to change what I do, and right now I get to do what I want to do!" His eyelids flickered, his cheeks fiery red.

"Right there is the original sin of Satan—pride, doing what *he* wanted instead of God's will."

"I'm not Satan," he said.

"Agreed, you are not he," I replied, nodding. He was getting mad. This needed to end soon.

"And I can still choose—"

"—to follow God's Truth or to follow your little truth, but in knowing Truth exists, do you not want it?"

"Maybe, but not now."

"Famous words of St. Augustine." I said, smiling. "Once you know there is an absolute truth, there is no going back to any relative truth that you want to be true."

"I think I understand that, but say it again, simpler." Bob was still listening. I was amazed.

"I know many people who do not understand the Catholic faith and therefore hate the falseness that she is not," I said, remembering something similar Scott Hahn had said, "but of those who really know their Catholic faith and the Truth that it is, there is no going back."

"You want to convert me?" he said, "I'm older than you are!"

"Yes, yes, I do, and you are," I replied. "But I cannot convert you. I can only plant a seed or two. The Holy Spirit and your free will must do the rest."

"I need to go now," he said, backing quickly away from me.

I reflected on how we can tell the truth, but people will run away. A sinner would rather you join them and wallow in their sin. When you point out their sin, they run to try to hide from the exposure it creates. Truth makes us feel naked as did Adam and Eve after biting the apple from the tree of knowledge. If only we accept truth and live truth, we are humbled, but we are not stripped naked.

While I feel the disappointment of those who chose to

hate truth, leave truth, run away from truth, I try to live out Christ's command to "shake the dust off our sandals" wherever He is not accepted. Still I follow His call for mercy and continue to pray and act with the desire to convert souls.

I must try to win souls for God. I continue to try, even when I know before starting a conversation that most likely the person will run away and stop communicating with me. I am flawed: failing more often than succeeding. The key, I believe, is to keep it up because no matter how many times I fall, God will help me get back up. The Sacrament of Confession can make even me, a sinner, as white as snow. This way, the only way really, I can get back up and try again and try to improve. I must have faith that the Holy Spirit will use me, and you, reader, and other people and other miraculous events to convert souls for God.

Chapter 23
Final Thoughts
2019

Three priests and a writer visited us in one week, each separately.

I wondered what God was preparing me for. Often when there is a gift like this, God knows hard times are coming. Right after they left, I began writing this autobiography. Sharing my personal story is just the beginning of my process of casting into the deep to catch many fish for God.

I am glad they visited me to fill me with strength. It was not all pleasant, as nothing is on earth. These men threw me into the snow, so to speak. They offered their reflections on my experiences of rejection and showed me how those were tools to better shape my soul. That week changed my life as I realized they loved me and, if they can love me, that I can love anyone.

While many chose to hate or dismiss me, I am still amazed by those who chose to love me. Many times, in my early life, I said and did things no one could love, and yet some loved me. In this way, we love others even more when they are hard to love. I thought back to loving Dad after a beating, loving my mom after a mental fit, and to those who loved me in all my weaknesses and flaws.

So, how do I keep loving people even when I am persecuted, beaten, mocked, and belittled? Well, there were the amazing people who kept loving me even in the worst times of my life. If others can love this sinner, how much more can we love those whom society would call unlovable, such as the outcast, the rejected, the imprisoned, the starving, the homeless, the drug addict, the thrice-abused and those without so-called rights such as the unborn, the elderly, the dying, the diseased, the disabled, and anyone who cannot speak out for him or herself?

How much more must we love those who are weak, as would not a parent love even more a child who is sick?

****

What I had failed to understand as an atheist was the unknown and the unknowable. There are areas of science where we do not have an answer…yet. I call that the unknown.

But there is also the unknowable. For example, who knows the mind of God, but God? God told us "I am Who am." Who knows my mind, but God and me? I am His and mine. And since I am flawed, do I really know my own mind and what I want? I do not know, but God does know my mind. So, that is the unknowable: topics where science has no ability to answer questions of philosophy, meaning, and purpose.

At one point, I became a student of the history of science. I found that Catholics were for science and technology. There were many monks, priests, nuns and laypeople that made important contributions to western science. Catholics for over 2000 years have been for the scientific method, for science, for technology, and for the common good of society. I came to realize that there is a marriage between faith and reason, that reason is the wings on which faith soars.

If you dig deep enough to understand the universe, you will find God. So, I encourage you to ask tough questions, to dig deep, to search and you will find, knock and the door will be opened for you. When you look at the top scientists, you find people of faith, people who believe there is something to be found. Many scientists are artistic. They work hard but are also creative, and having faith was an important part of their discovery process.

If you believe that you can only know what you see, just think of how many things you accept as real even though you cannot see them? Viruses, bacteria, mold, atoms, distant planets, ancient leaders, the list goes on and on of things that are believed even though we do not see them.

For example, do you know how your computer works? No? How about your cell phone? Video recorder? Yet, they do work, and we trust that they are real, even though we cannot see their workings, only their effects.

Consider the evidence in the universe, such as the gravitational constant and other constants of the universe. Move them just a little bit, and life no longer could exist in our universe. The probability of life in this universe is infinitesimally small, so small scientists were embarrassed when they realized just how unlikely it is. So, the idea of multiverses, other universes was invented. Even then, it would take trillions and trillions of universes just to get one like this.

If you believe there is an order to the universe, you

can have faith that you can find the order, and in finding that order, you can glimpse the face of God. The conflict then between faith and reason went away in my mind. As a former atheistic scientist, I have not seen anything in my field of science that contradicts the teachings of the Catholic Church in any way.

The other conflict that went away in my mind was the struggle for those who might not have had a good father role model. The biological father is the first example of our Heavenly Father. When that biological father is *not* such a great example to follow, it can be easy to confuse a father's poor behavior with God; that it somehow points to God being bad. But that is false. God is good. He is our adopted Heavenly Father - who loves even more those who are poor in spirit.

As a Catholic, I look at the world in an entirely different way than I did when I was an atheist. The change to me is earth-shattering.

I love everyone.

I see purpose in life.

I see purpose in suffering and even in death.

Going from an exhausted atheist to a joyful Catholic did not mean I had more material wealth as a Catholic or a better life as a Catholic. In fact, I suffer many of the same physical, mental, psychological, and spiritual afflictions as a Catholic that I did as an atheist.

So, if my life is not immediately and obviously better in a secular way, why bother to be Catholic? First, it is the Truth, and that matters in our consciousness, our heart, and our mind. Second, our entire lives are like a parable, a story for others to learn from, much like the Journey Home show on EWTN, and there is meaning and purpose to every second of our existence. Third, the only faith that understands life as we live it, including pain, suffering, and death, and explains those events is the Catholic Church.

My understanding of reality is more real as a Catholic than it was as an atheist. For example, my father died in April of 2015. Before he died, my father confessed and went to Mass. I pray for his soul and I hope he is in purgatory. I hope to be a good husband and father to my wife and six children, to give them the attention we all so badly need from our parents.

Around the same time my father passed away, my family found our half-sister (the daughter of my father and his second wife) and it is amazing getting to know her. I suppose I could have felt anger and resentment at these events, but as a Catholic they are put into a proper light.

Imagine a tapestry, and on the back side are all these strings garbled up together in bunches and knots.

What a mess.

But turn over the canvas and there is a beautiful mural.

God is making good and purpose from our lives and loves us even more when we suffer.

Do we not love our kids, students, nieces, nephews, friends, and new acquaintances even more when they are weak?

If so, imagine how much more our Heavenly Father loves us and plans for us an eternal joy in Heaven in His presence and the meaningfulness of the tapestry of the universe throughout time and space and beyond into the greater spiritual Kingdom of Heaven.

If you are in the darkness, or experiencing a dark night of the soul, although you may feel temporary comfort in hiding, I call you out of the darkness and into His glorious light.

No matter what you did, no matter what has happened to you, no matter how bad you feel, or think that you are without hope of recovery, do not be afraid of the light.

God already knows everything about you.

Walk out into His glorious light so that you may see yourself and others as we truly are: sinners who keep on trying.

If you are struggling between switching between the dark and the light, realize that no matter how many times I may fail, or you may fail, that God will never give up on trying to win us to His love as long as we live.

If you are already in the light, I call on you to bring others into the light. Pass along this book to those who need it more than you do. Be full of hope, a flagship full of candles for others to see in the fog of sin. Speak and act and pray that you may be an instrument of God to guide souls to Him. Do not give up hope, and if you are persecuted in His name, be full of joy.

May God bless you and keep you safe. Pray for me and I will pray for you. I hope that you, reader, and I, humble reporter of my life, may all return to God in His glorious joy forever and ever.

Amen.

Biblical Quotes

Called out of the Darkness into His Glorious light
1 Peter 2:9
But you are a chosen people, a royal priesthood, a holy nation, God's special possession, that
you may declare the praises of him who called you out of darkness into His marvelous [glorious] light.

Jesus Raises Lazarus John 11:42-43
I know that You always hear Me; but because of the people standing around I said it, so that they may believe that You sent Me. - John 11:42
The dead man [Lazarus] came out, his hands and feet wrapped with strips of linen, and a cloth around his face. Jesus said to them, "Take off the grave clothes and let him go." - John 11:43

Acknowledgments

I have attempted to preserve the dignity of people in this autobiography by changing names and altering locations so that persons are protected from identification. The identity of individuals does not have a relevant bearing on this work because my autobiography is about how I reverted to the Catholic faith, not about my judging any person.

I wish to personally thank those who helped make this book happen, including Marcus Grodi and the entire staff at the Coming Home Network. Our senior editor, Ellen Gable Hrkach, as well as editors, Patrice MacArthur, Katherine O'Brien, Lawrence Bilello III, and Kurt Johnson who worked tirelessly to improve the story. Our creative artist James Hrkach who nailed the cover on his first try. Our marketing permission team at my alumni Northwestern University for copyright clearance use of names of places and streets. The members of the Garden Club of Evanston for providing a high-quality photograph and permission to reproduce the Shakespeare Garden picture for our back cover. This Evanston campus garden played an important role in changing my direction in life.

A special thank you to all the people who have prayed for me and acted on my spiritual behalf. Among the cloud of witnesses are those on Earth: my lovely wife and all my dear children, my vulnerable mother, my prayerful sisters and brothers, all my friends and acquaintances; and those suffering in purgatory and those triumphant in Heaven: especially to Joseph, Mary, Jesus, the Holy Spirit and the Father.

As much as possible, I tried to take myself lightly and be humbled for your benefit. This book is dedicated to you, the reader, that some part of my story may become as a parable in your heart, to help you in some small way so that the Holy Spirit may act on you and others in a big way.

About the Author

Dr. Paul Keough holds an MBA in Finance from the University of Michigan's Ross School of Business and a Ph.D. in Health Sciences from Northwestern University. Paul is a practicing Catholic husband and father of six children who attend Catholic schools in the western suburbs of Chicago. In his free time, Paul enjoys playing chess and stays active by biking, swimming, playing basketball and tennis and working out with his family and friends.

Career-wise, Paul initially worked on Wall Street with high-profile investors, but then Dr. Keough soon realized his true passion was for helping individuals and their families on Main Street grow their retirement funds. Paul left Wall Street to help the average Joe and Jane on Main Street. Dr Keough brought with him the same experiences and knowledge that he used to research investments for the affluent. Since then, Paul has remained focused on helping his clients work toward their retirement dreams.

Dr. Keough has been recognized for his dedication to clients and featured in the media, most notably, on EWTN's *The Journey Home* that aired January 2016:

http://bit.ly/2h9wNBS

or heard me speak on Dan Cheely's Relevant Radio Show in April 2016:

http://bit.ly/2znOVCc

Recently in December 2017, Paul was interviewed by the podcast SeizeYourBusiness.com as episode 132: "The Information War & Emotional Finance:"

http://bit.ly/2ja9Mzu

Also, on Dec 22nd of 2018, Paul was interviewed on Montréal CAN Radio Blog:

https://youtu.be/fUW59xS_2_4"

Paul is currently the Principal and Chief Compliance Officer (CCO) of Turnkeough Wealth Management, Inc., where he supervises all activities of the firm. Paul adheres to applicable regulatory requirements, together with all policies and procedures outlined in the firm's code of ethics and compliance manual. He holds a Series 65 securities license and earned his health and life insurance license in multiple states throughout the United States.

Turnkeough Wealth Management, Inc. is a Registered Investment Advisor Firm with trades executed through Pershing LLC, Member FINRA, NFA & SIPC. Our disclosures are that past performance is not indicative of future performance and all proforma activities including forecasts are forward-looking estimates and are not guarantees of performance. Any risk mitigation is partial, some risks always remain, and risks are usually proportional to potential return regardless of mitigations.

The approach at Turnkeough is unusual for a wealth management firm. First, they have a mission statement to provide comprehensive life planning. When Paul meets with investors, he asks over 300 questions in three hours in these areas: investments, insurance, estate, education, debt, retirement, legal, tax, real estate, career, marriage, spiritual,

family and legacy planning.
Their holistic approach is designed to build confidence and comfort. Their goal is to be a good and loyal servant to each of their clients, offering to help with both their clients' communities' long-term benefit and the benefit of the clients' loved ones. The firm is resolutely committed to serving Christians and Jews by providing honest, caring, and thoughtful professional services. They hold seriously the higher standards of always telling the truth, providing flawless service, minimizing costs, while providing top notch services with kindness and a smile.

The firm abides by compliance, recordkeeping, and regulations, manages and tracks performance and results. But also, they hold themselves to a higher standard. The firm has an ethical board of directors composed of non-voting religious persons.

Turnkeough also tithes and gives to various not-for-profit causes all over the world. "We encourage our team to give and when I'm asked how much I say give, give, give until it hurts and then give some more."

The firm is also very competitive with other financial firms by offerings services where client goals come first always, by seeking alpha (return above market return), keeping costs low using trading methods, providing real attention and real analysis, without automated robots with the goal of exceeding their clients' expectations.

For further information, please contact Dr. Keough at:

www.turnkeough.com
Executive Towers West
1431 Opus Pl. Unit 110
Downers Grove, IL 60515
paul.keough@turnkeough.com
Office: 1-630-796-3922